Original Sin

A God-Soul Theory

Edward Conklin Ph.D.

ISBN 978-0-9988338-3-5

Dedication

I dedicate this work to the young, who not told, usually must find out the hard way. I also dedicate the work to the brave few who through history explored body and brain and faithfully went where truth led them. Their words continue to resound through time, especially Akhenaton the heretic pharaoh of Egypt and prescient seer of modern times, and Jean Meslier the curate philosopher of France.

Acknowledgments

I owe my biological life to my parents and family generations. I acknowledge and especially thank my religious mother and my pagan father who provided a contrast of values and provided a sufficient amount of both comfort and discomfort to influence my early years. My psychological and philosophical orientation to life I owe in great part to my teacher, Dr. Amiya Chakravarty (1901-1986). Though I do not know if he would agree with my views, I certainly owe him my heartfelt appreciation for inspiring me to think more deeply about life and the human condition.

Published works by Edward Conklin Ph.D.

Original Sin: A God-Soul Theory. (2018). Amazon Kindle and CreateSpace.

God-Soul Theory for the 21st Century. (2017). Amazon Kindle and CreateSpace.

Psychology of God and the Soul. (2016). Amazon Kindle and CreateSpace.

Meditations on God and the Soul. (2015). Amazon Kindle and CreateSpace.

A Brief Guide to God and the Soul. (2015). Amazon Kindle and CreateSpace.

In the Beginning: A New Theory of the First Religion. (2014). Amazon Kindle and CreateSpace.

Cosmos, God, and Soul. (2014). Amazon Kindle and CreateSpace.

From Tool-maker to God Maker. (2014). Amazon Kindle and CreateSpace.

Waves Rough and Smooth & the Deep Blue Sea. (2014). Amazon Kindle and CreateSpace.

Getting Back Into the Garden of Eden. (1998). University Press of America.

Introduction

As most do when young, I pondered on what to dedicate my life to. Eventually, due to a lack of practical ability and talent, I found a path less traveled and chose to parlay an innate psychological acumen to investigate religion.

Two areas of long-term and abiding interest to humankind are a monotheistic god and an animating soul of life. Many individuals proceed through life relying on nominal faith and personal belief, and trust in the traditions of monotheistic religions. However, it is more realistic and rewarding to explore the psychological dynamic of two areas of investigation, and to bring some reasonable clarity to the speculation and mystery of a first father god and what animates life.

Unsought but guided by a thin thread of fate through a lifelong strand of passing years, unintended and unbeknownst, life developed into a psychological investigation of a first father god and a soul that survives physical death. The work has been both a burden and a blessing but there are few regrets to having spent some precious years of swift-passing life investigating the twin topics of a monotheistic god and the ancient notion of an animating soul. The result of these labors is the God-Soul Theory.

The theory asserts that a first father god exists only subjectively and psychologically and not objectively. Skeptics will argue that a monotheistic god and a soul exist beyond the ability of human comprehension and so cannot be better known. I argue that the dynamic of both a first father god and the animating soul of life can be reasonably better defined and known.

The evolving restless human brain/mind is unceasing in its quest to comprehend what is real and true and what is not. Most people are too busy living daily life and have precious little time to ask questions, to seek and to find, and to better comprehend. Many must live life accepting what is false and seem to be no less the worse for doing so. For these people, only the living of life matters. Yet a few individuals require more comprehension.

Knowledge and wisdom usually take a back seat to the daily tasks of living. However, the Greek philosopher Socrates (469-399 BCE) made the statement, "The unexamined life is not worth living." I expand on Socrates urging to acquire philosophical and psychological wisdom, and say further that a deep need long exists for humankind to better comprehend the first father god of monotheism, and the soul that animates life. What follows is a collection of essays that explore the dynamic of these two topics. The work is a theological exposé of the psychological dynamic of a first father god and an animating soul.

Millennium

A millennium is a measure of a thousand years and the time span is prominent in the religions of Zoroastrianism, Buddhism, Christianity and Bahia. Approximately 8,000 millennia ago, originating from the environment, primate forebears of modern humans began a long evolving development. Recently in the year 2000 CE, humankind entered a new millennium that will stretch through the distant years to 3000 CE.

For approximately two and one-half millennia, monotheistic religions have advocated the view of humans as sinful and separate from goodness, conceived to be a first father god. There has been an egregious separation but this has been the result of monotheistic religions who imaginatively and artistically trace the origin of the environment and life to a good first father god. This effectively separates life from its real origin of a good and evil environment.

The notion of a monotheistic first father god will be seen at some point during the now elapsing millennium, as a quaint stage of ancestor worship in the evolving maturation and future cognitive development of humankind. The time of pragmatic usefulness and influence of monotheism is now fading, and at some time during the new millennium, will expire completely.

Monotheistic religions began a mere two and one-half millennia ago, and during this time their teachings have been both helpful and harmful to the endeavors of humankind. While a first father god certainly confers some benefits to humankind, a future deicide is inevitable. The eventual comprehension that life is a continuation of the energy particles of the environment will bestow a beneficial clarity to human existence. During the coming millennium, monotheistic religions will reach the end of their long supportive role of Middle Eastern and Western cultures.

Monotheistic religions with their insistence on the existence of a first father god, are increasingly incompatible with modern findings of biology, cosmology, physics, and psychology.

The cerebral cortex of the human brain seeks to improve life experience. It does this by reasoning, research, inventiveness, and theoretical and applied sciences. The cerebral cortex can also improve life through artistic expression. Both kinds of differing efforts and products contribute to improving the quality of living.

In modern times, there exist two competing theories for the origin of existence, the artistic and the scientific. The artistic theory is the monotheistic word portrait of a first father god as portrayed in Jewish, Christian, and Islamic literary stories. In these monotheistic scriptures, a first father god is portrayed as the origin of the environment and the animator of life. The human-like beginning spoken of in monotheistic writings, is a simplistic and artistic way to identify the origin of existence. No difficult mathematics or science is required when using the verbal and written art of story to identify how the environment and life came to exist.

The twentieth and twenty-first century empirical sciences are slowly and surely reducing the influence of the artistic religious theory of a first father god that is accepted by many to be the origin of the environment and life. Monotheistic religions no longer serve as a viable and reliable explanation of why humans are separate from a higher good in life. The God-Soul Theory serves as a much better and more realistic model of humankind's place in the universe.

God-Soul Theory

Truth can be found in either/or explanations but is also just as often discovered midway between two alternatives. Such is the solution to the question, does a monotheistic first father god exist? The God-Soul Theory answers the conundrum by affirming yes, a first father does exist as a subjective imaginal idea in the cerebral cortex of the human brain but does not exist objectively as real and true. A first father god exists only subjectively and is therefore only half real. The God-Soul Theory advocates for a psychological view of partial-atheism. The theory asserts that a first father god is subjectively real to a sizable group of humans but the personal acceptance and belief of many is no guarantee that it is objectively real.

A monotheistic god is a subjective and prescientific way of identifying an unknown beginning, and is an imagined artistic way of orienting to what is good and protective of humans. The first father god of monotheism is derived not from reasoning, as suggested and accepted in the past but is instead a product of artistic imagining and story, as an effort to know an unknown beginning of the environment and life.

The God-Soul Theory also asserts that since a first father is an expression of human ability for artistic imagining and word art, a popular yet poorly conceived notion of a human soul cannot have been made by and has nothing to do with a human-like god. An animating soul is a continuation of the natural environment of energy and force and it is this factor that renders it resistant to destruction. The soul is a triune forceful function of hunger for food and water, sex and reproduction, and aggression that enables life to survive and is resistant to destruction.

Survival

A first father god is praised as the beginning of existence and is looked to as an ancestor who can regulate reality and the many out of control events that affect human lives. Praise be for a regulator and regulations to better survive life. Human knowledge is often insufficient to regulate human willing and to direct it to good and away from use of the excessive force known as evil. A first father portrayed in the monotheistic word art of story is the attempt to regulate behavior from outside of the human body, by artistically and subjectively imagining the god inside the cerebral cortex of the brain.

The artistic imagining and clinging to a monotheistic scriptural word portrait of a first father god is an emotional and psychological mechanism of a willing determination to survive life experience and death of the body. Monotheistic religions accept and believe the notion that the physical body will be resurrected and saved by a first father. The Christian religion also appeals to the human need to survive with the offer of a first father, and unlike the other monotheistic religions, also offers a savior son of the god.

The artistically imagined first father god or a begotten son to save a person is not needed, as the body is a continuation of real force and energy. There will be a default save of an animating soul to survive supported by what it is a continuation of, atoms and electrons of energy and a cosmological force.

The monotheistic use of the generic word god, refers to the origin of what is both inside and outside of the body. The word denotes an external first father and how the body is animated from the outside. The use of the word also refers to where the god really originates, the subjective intelligent function of the human cerebral cortex of the brain, and its creative imagining of an external first father to be the origin of existence.

The biblical Genesis story of the origin of existence is treated by many as objective history, when it is a subjectively imagined artistic story of word art. A first father god creatively imagined to be good, exists only in artistic story and words. To say that a monotheistic first father is good, does not to refer to what is objective but is to really say that god is a good idea. A first father god is a subjectively good idea as it quickly and simply identifies the beginning of existence. If the beginning of existence is intelligent it can intend and provide care and protection for humans in life and after death as a wished-for resurrection of the body.

To better survive life, monotheistic word artists imagine stories of a first father god to assist humans Having made the earth and weather events, the forefather can be implored to control the environment. The pragmatically imagined first father also serves to impose ethical and moral authority and obedience over individuals of a society. Lacking a strong benevolent real human leader, only an artistically imagined all-powerful animating first father god is capable of imposing order on the environment and on argumentative and conflict prone humans. What assists biological life to survive is not an imagined helper god but a real soul. The real origin of human life is not a first father god but a sensed yet usually unidentified or misidentified animating soul. In the scriptures of monotheistic religions, only a god gets credit for animating life, and later a touting of a body resurrection. There is no mention of an animating soul.

In popular thinking, the soul is usually identified as associated with a first father god. The soul is not identified as being a continuation of element energies from the earth, and the environment is usually not identified as a continuation of a cosmological force that moves the universe. As a continuation of energy and force, if the soul can be said to be caring, it cares only to exist and survive as befits its attribute of being resistant to destruction.

Monotheistic religions subjectively insist that a first father god exists. It must be recognized and accepted that only a nonhuman objective origin is real. Inside the human body is a real animating triune soul as a hunger for food and water, sex and reproduction, and aggression. The soul is a continuation of real quantum particles, atoms, and electron energy elements of the earth, and an omnipresent surround of a cosmological force that moves the universe and ever exists on its own.

In the biblical Genesis story, the animator of life is not the real environment but is an imagined story character of a first father god who stooped to use the red soil of the lowly earth to form the first human. Real life is formed not by a first father god but is an evolving continuation from a real external supporting environment of circular atom and electron energy elements. This process is continued as an internal function that forcibly forms and animates cellular life to survive as an innate hunger for food and water, sex and reproduction, and aggression.

Within the conscious cerebral cortex of the brain, survival is facilitated by perception, reasoning, measuring, and inventing tools and weapons. Survival is also facilitated by conception and by artistically imagining a word story of a first father. Utilizing an evolved innate ability to imagine, biblical word artists inflated human intelligence to the extraordinary level of a first father god.

In monotheistic religions, creative storytellers imagine a first father god and extend it outward from its internal cerebral cortex of the brain origin to the past as a simple artistic way to identify the beginning of existence.

Once Upon A Time

Once upon a time, circa twenty-five hundred years ago, Judaic and Israelite seekers strained their brains to know the beginning of the environment and life. What eventually transpired is that biblical word artists, inspired on the inside of their cerebral cortex of the brain, imagined the existence of a first father and expired it outward. The rationale must have been, why tolerate an unknown beginning, and why be helpless when the beginning can easily be imagined and spoken of to be a first father god who made existence and who can help humans?

Through the previous two and one-half millennia to the twenty-first century, the artistic monotheistic word rendering of a first father origin has been generally accepted and regarded by adherents as actually real and existent. Worship of a monotheistic first father god, is really worship of a long line of sexual reproduction by forefathers. The story of a first father god is an imagined substitute for the real biological sexual reproduction process of many forefathers and mothers. Having faith in a helping first father is a long wait, as in reality it is merely faith in the ability of forefathers to sexually reproduce and bring forth human life.

The monotheistic way of directing human attention to what is better behavior in life, is accomplished by portraying a first father as dictating commandments to be obeyed. The imagined rational personality of a first father god also represents a moral authority to command the irrational subconscious urges of human sexual reproduction and aggression. Human willing is often irrational, so the first father god makes his extra-rational willing known through verbal and written commands as a way of directing and guiding individuals of a monotheistic culture. Humans appeal to a subjectively conceived first father god to manage life but must really manage all on their own. Humans must manage as best as they can, the environment, other life forms, and fellow humans.

The word artists of the opening chapters of the book of Genesis, project an intelligence to exist prior to the environment and life, and is imagined to be a first father who is then portrayed in story as an all-knowing god who made existence.

A strong and good monotheistic first father god is artistically imagined and projected from the creative confines of the cerebral cortex of the brain in an effort to counter a real dualistic good and evil environment. A first father god occurs only and exclusively as a subjective idea imagined in the conscious cerebral cortex of the brain.

Biblical authors could not and did not employ the methods of mathematics or observation of empirical science to explore reality. The only other recourse to make known the beginning of existence during the time, was to make use of artistic imagination and to verbally sketch a word portrait in written story format. A first father god is a word artist rendition, an artistic imaginal word rendering of the beginning of existence. Biblical word artists originated the fanciful idea of a first father and then verbally elaborated and designed it with words to be a supernatural god. Through story, biblical word artists deified the beginning of existence to be a first father god. This is a process that occurs only in the cerebral cortex of the human brain that projects and attributes its own intelligence to come from a more intelligent external first father god.

If the beginning of the environment and life was to remain unidentified and unknown, or not intelligent, humans must then bear the full burden of relying on their own often deficient intelligence. Worry and woe would certainly be the result for humankind, as the conscious cerebral cortex of the brain would experience an excess of existential angst and despair. An imagined first father god lightens the burden and daily struggle of living.

First Father

Using the metaphor of a train, humans are on a track of time, laid down by ancestors of the past and continuing in every now moment. Humans are laying track as they go, fast or slow.

Some in the past and many today have the view there is an invisible track-maker, a first father god who puts humans on a track of life known as predestination.

Lacking mathematics and science, primitive people creatively identified the origin of the environment and life by imagining a story. The monotheistic artistic word portrait extends back in time to a beginning made by a first father god. The way open for biblical writers to reveal the origin of existence, was to use artistic imagination to craft a story that describes the adventures of a first father ancestor.

The monotheistic story of a first father god is a metaphor for a collective of real biological fathers, and mothers. To trace human origin to a first father is to utilize a metaphorical image for the sexual behavior and reproduction of forefathers, and a concomitant and continual hunger for and finding of food and water, and the aggressive behaviors of killing animals and fellow humans. To imagine and label an unknown beginning of countless acts of sexual reproduction to be a first father god is a real delusion. Having faith in a helping first father is a long wait, as in reality it is merely faith in the ability of forefathers to sexually reproduce and bring forth human life.

Visage

The hunger for and finding of food and water is a bodily act, as is sex and reproduction, and aggression. The human cerebral cortex evaluates any unruly body functions and behaviors, and disapproves of them. Dismayed by the human condition, the cerebral cortex of the brain may then imagine the external visage of a first father god as a way of obtaining assistance in the ongoing human drama of life. The artistic imagining of a first father is a subjective way of identifying the origin of existence, and the god is also a way to preside over and to instill and enforce individual and social obedience.

A first father god is a visage fashioned by word artisans and placed over the poorly comprehended cosmological motion of the universe, energy, solar system, and the animation of life. For some years now in Middle East and Western cultures, the unhuman-like universe has worn the visage of a monotheistic first father god.

Fashioned by words, the visage of an overseeing first father functions to identify the origin of existence, and to reduce fear of a mostly unknown and uncaring universe.

Members of monotheistic religions meet to praise a first father god. More realistically, they are meeting to praise their own higher cerebral cortex of the brain that imagines the ideational visage of a first father ancestor. Monotheists meet and bask in their ability to have the highest attitude toward others, and to recognize a common shared forefather elevated to the stature of a god. This is worship of the human conscious self, under the guise of the greater imagined ego of a first father god.

When monotheists meet to praise a first father, they are realistically meeting to praise their mutual use of the higher cerebral cortex of the brain, the site of imagining the visage of a shared god. The cerebral cortex is the site of higher ethical and moral attitudes toward fellow humans. Any lower attitudes and behaviors are, not without effort, at least temporarily inhibited by the higher cerebral cortex.

Unfortunately, most monotheists continue to unanimously agree to not ever relinquish the subjective artistic way of looking at the origin of the universe. Sadly, members of monotheistic religions all agree and stubbornly insist that the universe must forever have the visage of a first father god. Eventually though, the stubborn monotheistic faith and trust in the artistic word portrait of a first father god, will like all things deteriorate through time.

Celebrity

A monotheistic first father is an artistic embellishment, a word portrait of fictional story details. The god is an imagined celebrity, puffed up to exist and to perform not in external reality but only on the conscious internal stage of the cerebral cortex of the brain. A first father is a monotheistic celebrity, an imagined famous actor projected on the screen of conscious human attention. The cerebral cortex projects and pretends a first father to exist on the stage of existence. The actor appears not as a visual image but is produced as a word portrait.

The first father is famed while the environment and an animating human soul are defamed by not being recognized as the real origin of life.

Sideshow

A sideshow is defined as:

"A small show offered in addition to the main attraction, as in a circus. A diversion or spectacle incidental to a larger set of circumstances or conditions. A subordinate show of little importance relative to a larger or main event. The act of exhibiting or entertaining the public, a demonstration or show of skill."

The monotheistic story of a first father origin is a public sideshow in the circus that is life. The character of a Sideshow God, serves as a small cultural human diversion and distraction from a real vast scene of universal motion ever moved by a cosmological force. The story of a first father god is a small sideshow distraction from the near environment of sun, earth, and weather, and the main attraction of an immense aesthetic of distant galaxies and stars. Monotheistic word artists exhibit the word portrait of a first father god to entertain the public during religious services. Monotheistic authorities demonstrate their knowledge of having personal knowledge of the origin of existence and also their skill of communicating with the god.

A first father is usually considered to be the primary show of the universe while a pleasing environment is secondary and usually considered to be evidence only of the god's aesthetic creativity. The main event of the real universe is overlooked as well as its continuation of what animates life within, not as an external first father animator but what immediately grows life as an internal animating soul.

Message to Monotheists

To the many monotheists who worship a first father god, consider the following message.

Wherever you may be, in a group or individually, when you worship a first father, what you really do is to bow your head to a long line of male ancestor sexual reproduction, which is what the artistically imagined god in great part represents.

Misguided by tradition and lack of knowledge, you direct your subjective attention to a higher intelligence to comfort and save you, and mistake it to be an objective first father. The god is really a subjective idea that resides in the cerebral cortex of the human brain. You read the artistically imagined and crafted fictional word portrait scriptures and feel comforted, at least for a time.

When considering dying and death, you take refuge in a first father god. Yet the god is a subjective representation, an agreed upon way of imagining a cause of the environment and life. The god is a way of encapsulating you and to protect you from the unknown and any potential harm. Your subjectively imagined big palooka of a first father obscures a real origin from the environment, the objective biological act of sexual reproduction, and a long line of biological evolution.

Subjective Comfort

Ideas do not have to be objectively true; they can function to benefit only subjective comfort and pleasure. Such is the word art portrait of a first father portrayed by monotheistic religions. The portrait of a monotheistic god is not sculpted nor painted, but is rendered apparent to conscious comprehension by using the word art of story.

A first father god is a subjective idea of good that makes some humans feel good. In the real, good and evil experiences of life, the imaginal idea of a first father god is a way to direct attention to what is good and can help humans, and away from bad and evil situations that can often render them helpless. Not to have the conscious idea of a first father god, many humans would not know the origin of existence, would be vulnerable to harm, and will encounter ageing and death alone or in the company of other crying and frightened relatives and friends.

The subjective idea of a god helps to comprehend the unknown, and helps as an ideational refuge of good from the evils of living and dying.

Not a first father god but elements of energy of the environment and earth is the real maker and supporter of life. The real animating energy and willing-like change of the environment is not identified to be the origin of life. Instead, an artistic word portrait of a first father god gets credit for the process. Attention is directed to the past, to artistically imagine and deposit a first father of previous forefathers. When human willing is ineffective, attention is directed by many to the greater willing of an imaginal first father god who can assist humans in their often helpless situations of living.

The conscious reasoning cerebral cortex of the brain, also known as the self, has its limits interacting with the less conscious and subconscious midbrain and body functions, also known as an animating and willing triune soul of hunger for food and water, sex and reproduction, and aggression. The less conscious and subconscious animating soul function of midbrain and body is a problem for the conscious self of the cerebral cortex of the brain. The conscious self glorifies its own functions of reasoning and picture images to be the soul of life. Or the conscious self glorifies its existence by imagining a first father god from whence it has an origin.

A first father god is imagined by the cerebral cortex of the brain to save humans but this is a delusion made into the word art of monotheistic story. It is the animating soul that saves humans, whether they want, or do not want to be saved. The first father artistic subjective delusion by the cerebral cortex of the brain, is accepted rather than observing an internal animating soul to be resistant to destruction as it is a continuation of energy particles of a supportive environment.

Happiness

The chore of obtaining human happiness falls mainly to the conscious cerebral cortex of the brain.

To reduce and remove the unhappiness of not knowing the beginning of existence, the cerebral cortex imagines a first father god. To reduce the unhappiness of living, the cerebral cortex imagines a first father who cares and protects, and this makes many humans subjectively happy.

For many, a first father god is a role model for happiness. The first father does not hunger for food, and though making humans in his image (Genesis 1:26-27) and therefore must have genitals, does not have sex and reproduce, and while not generally harming humans, does often curse, punish, and kill them at times. Therefore, it may be imagined that the monotheistic first father must be reasonably happy. Unfortunately, for humans, they must struggle to remove unhappiness and to retain what little happiness they can obtain, and this is subject to change. If a first father god is happy, despite many unhappy personal experiences, humans can also aspire to happiness. Imagining a first father god makes existence safer during life and death, and therefore produces a modicum of human happiness.

The Wall

The Western or Wailing Wall in Jerusalem, is a foundation wall and support for the Temple Mount where the Jewish Temple was once located. The base wall is all that remains of the Temple site. The significance of touching and praying at the Wall today, is a way of touching the past when the Jewish Temple existed prior to its destruction by the Romans in 70 CE. Touching the wall stones is also a symbolic way of touching the solid support and strength of an imagined artistic word portrait of a first father god. (1 Samuel 2:2; Psalms 18:2; 1 Peter 2:4-8)

The rock wall of hard limestone may also symbolize the obdurate will of worshippers to endure existence with the hardened and strong stone of subjective faith. A first father god is appealed and prayed to. Realistically, a first father only represents the imagined extreme terminus of many sexual acts of biological reproduction in the distant past.

Over the previous two millennia, the monotheistic concept of a god has hardened and become an obdurate willing to survive for whomever subscribes to the religion. Individual willpower hardens to cling to the primitive, simplistic, and subjective notion of a monotheistic first father god.

Buildings

The buildings of monotheistic religions dot the landscape in the Middle East, Europe, and Western countries; they exist to denote the importance of identifying where the environment and life comes from. They are places to comprehend the beginning, artistically portrayed in word art as a first father god. Monotheistic word art offers comprehension of the origin of existence, and also seeks to direct human attention to better ethical and moral behaviors. Individuals are exposed to the idea of a first father god through reading or hearing about it. Susceptible individuals then accept the ideology on faith, shared belief, and trust in group tradition.

A monotheistic building represents the builder of the environment and life. In a real error, the builder of life is artistically imagined and misrepresented to be a first father god. The real generally sensed but misapprehended builder of life is the energy of a supportive earth, and a continuation of it as an internal animating triune soul of hunger for food and water, sex and reproduction, and aggression.

In modern times, monotheistic buildings are being replaced by buildings that house the laboratories of research, applied, and theoretical sciences, for example, physics that investigates energy particles, neuroscience and genetics that study brain and body functions. Science continues to make many evidential advances in knowledge, yet many people continue to be skeptical of science and its reliance on the fallible human cerebral cortex of the brain. More healthy skepticism and examination must instead be directed to the cerebral cortex of the brain that artistically imagines a monotheistic first father god.

Head Covering

Some individuals wear a cap or hat to cover their head as protection from the weather and sun, or for style and enjoyment. Similarly, monotheistic believers feel the need to cover themselves overhead with the imaginal idea in their own head of a first father, who if one can get the god's attention, will protect the head and body of the individual. Many individuals imagine a first father god to be located overhead as a protective covering during life and after death. The god said to be objectively overhead, exists only as a subjective idea inside the human head.

An example of this dynamic is illustrated by conservative and orthodox Jewish adherents who wear a head covering known as a *yarmulke*. Adherents of Jewish religion cover their heads in deference to the subjectively carried artistic imaginal first father god in their own head. A first father god cannot be found objectively but only subjectively as a word portrait in the Tanak. Monotheistic Christianity and Islam do not require a material head covering but do insist on the faith of carrying the imaginal idea of a first father god in their collective heads.

Bubble

The phrase and sentiment that "God is within" found in the religions of both Hinduism and Christianity is true but not as an animating factor, only as an artistic image or idea of a first father god formed and elaborated on in the cerebral cortex of the human brain. The first father god of monotheism, is an artistic overlay subjectively imagined to be objectively real.

Monotheistic religions inflate human intelligence and extend it outward to form the greater ego and protective bubble of a first father god. By this imaginal artistic maneuver, those who accept the view of a first father then place themselves inside the fragile brain-generated bubble of protection. The tensile bubble shape of imaginal protection must be maintained by keeping it inflated with frequent puffing of faith in thoughts and words of prayer to the god.

A first father god is artistically imagined, to reinforce the daily general pragmatic knowledge of the cerebral cortex of the brain.

A first father is a creative ploy to rationalize the difficult to control non-rational external environment and the internal irrational forces of the midbrain and body behaviors, also known as the animating soul of life, as hunger, sexuality, and aggression.

The Catholic sacrament of confession utilizes a first father god to reduce the guilt formed by personal sexual and aggressive behaviors. Forgiveness is attributed to a monotheistic first father when it is really the conscious cerebral cortex function of conscience that is appeased following confession, and consequently ceases to punish the individual with guilt and regret.

Only in recent times did Sigmund Freud (1865-1939) find that conscious inhibitory suppression and subconscious repression of sexuality and aggression result in psychological disorders. Freud found a way to remedy the guilt and conscience problems of fellow humans, not for a godly donation but for a goodly fee. Through trial and error observation, Freud developed his profitable unblocking of psychological resistance and conflict through the methods of free association and psychoanalysis.

The self-inflated bubble of the individual ego was pragmatically reduced to a manageable ordered level without the intervention and forgiveness of the imagined protective brain bubble of a first father god. Seeking to remove an individual's mistaken ideas or delusions, while profitable for psychoanalysts, can also be a risky business, resulting in resistance and even escalating into verbal and physical aggression.

Attempting to remove the cognitive error of monotheism and its first father god, is also both difficult and dangerous, resulting in religious conflicts and wars. Religious wars are really fought over artistic differences of word art, how a culture subjectively imagines and portrays the beginning of existence and life. Conflict is especially prevalent among the monotheistic Middle East religions of Judaism, Christianity, and Islam based on writings that artistically differ in portraying the word portrait of a first father god.

All names of monotheistic gods, such as Elohim, Yhwh, Alaha, and Allah, are pseudonyms for the real cerebral cortex of the brain that artistically imagines them.

Refuge

Life is a search to find ways to reduce struggle with what is outside and with what is inside the brain and body. The essential dynamic of life is the struggle to get what is wanted and to be away from what is not wanted.

There is a mental struggle, and a physical struggle to learn and to comprehend. Failing to reach an optimum by comprehending the environment and life, was for some cultures to result in the artistically imagined first father god of monotheism.

To seek refuge in a higher external reasoning, is to really take refuge in the internal subjective idea of a first father god located in the cerebral cortex of the brain. Refuge is sought from the unreasoning external environment, and from the internal less reasoning subconscious midbrain and body, the dynamic of which is a forcible animating triune soul of hunger for food and water, sex and reproduction, and aggression.

The first father god of monotheism is artistically imagined and intended to function as a refuge, a way to reduce struggle, desperation, and the despair of living and dying. The first father of all fathers is appealed to for emotional support. Emotion intended for a real supportive biological father, is instead diverted to an imaginal helpful first father god.

The subjective psychological act of imagining a first father god, is intended to remove the individual from experiences of frustration and pain, and may do so at least temporarily, to a place of supportive comfort. When a person prays and beseeches for intervention by a higher presence, what they really do is implement a higher attitude and search for a better comprehension of reason or intuition within their own cerebral cortex of the brain.

To say that god is good, does not to refer to what is objective but is to really say that god is a good subjective idea. Want to know where the environment and life comes from? Well, the simple answer spoon-fed to a curious individual is, a first father made all things. Want to know where to find care and protection during life and what awaits after death? A first father god is the simple and shallow answer to a personal quandary. The cerebral cortex of the brain imagines a first father, perched high in the sky above and beyond relative will-like changes of a night and day environment, and weather events.

The inexorable changes of the environment is imagined to be controlled by a god who made it with words. The simple notion of a first father god has such a utilitarian function, it is difficult to dissuade others that it only exists subjectively. The real lights of sun, moon, and stars illuminate darkness, while the imagined light of a first father god, faintly and superficially yet pragmatically, illuminates the dark times of human gloom, despair, and helplessness.

The only real refuge in the universe is the cerebral cortex of the human brain that both reasons and invents, and also artistically imagines a first father god. A first father is an artistic way of finding refuge from often poor reasoning and lesser human intelligence. The refuge of a higher intelligence is artistically imagined and elaborated on with words and projected to be a first father who made the environment and life. Monotheism is a simple and mistaken story that has evolved into a long term acceptable and traditional cultural delusion.

Word Art

Most religions utilize the arts of architecture, painting, sculpture, and music, to portray and to emphasize their various gods. Monotheistic religions also make use of some or all of these arts but prefers and especially utilizes the artistic medium of words to produce a verbal and written portrait of a first father god. The imaginal portrait appeals primarily to the young, and to unthinking and gullible adults.

Monotheism emphasizes belief, faith, and tradition, and therefore of necessity does not encourage methods of investigation that facilitate and promote self and soul exploration of brain and body functions.

That there is even talk of a first father is convincing evidence that most individuals are immature and have little comprehension. Monotheistic religions continue to insist on the janky conception and existence of a first father god. By imagining a first father, monotheistic religions exploit natural feelings for a real biological father. If an individual does not have a biological father, the person may experience sadness and loneliness, and therefore seek for a father figure or older friend.

A person may dwell on the memory of a missing or deceased father, or may live a sad and lonely existence by willful misconduct toward a father. This psychological cluster of ambivalent emotions and thoughts toward a biological father, may dispose a person to be easily exploited to accept a monotheistic imagined first father god. If taught by tradition to do so, a troubled person may turn to a fatherly god for relief. Reverence, respect, and thankfulness directed to a first father who made the environment and life, also reflects and shines back onto human males. The luster of the male ego is brightened as a result.

Many accept that surely something cared enough to make the environment and life. In artistic story, the unknown beginning was made known by imagining it to be a first father who therefore must care for humans. An artistic first father beginning is an image that simultaneously both represents and obscures the multiple sexual acts of many biological fathers on the earth. The good god represents the good pleasure of sexual orgasm of many previous forefathers, and the good and evil ambivalence of reproduction.

The efforts of monotheistic religions long continue to encourage humans to use their cerebral cortex of the brain to both accept the idea of a first father god, and to think about and do ethical and moral good. Monotheism seeks to convince followers that the subjective idea of a good first father god is real and exists objectively. The required vaunted faith to do so is but a wish to identify the beginning, and to obtain care and protection on a good and evil earth.

Just as a first father good god is an artistic imaginal story image illustrated with words, so are the human-like evil personalities of the subtle serpent of Genesis, Ahriman, Satan, Devil, Lucifer, and Iblis. Just as a good and loving first father god is subjectively imagined to exist, so too these entities are subjective works of word and visual art as a way of identifying the cause of what is bad and evil.

A monotheistic first father god is not real except as a subjective work of art, a word portrait in story held up to human attention as a pragmatic tool utilized by authority figures to inspire needy individuals. With the artistic use of words, monotheistic authors and authority figures convert susceptible individuals to the artistic view of a first father god. The stories of monotheism are an artistic expression of story images that sketch a first father portrait using letters and words. The monotheistic story of a first father god is a vague abstract outline, a work of art traced and sketched with mere words. The word stories of monotheism are perceived accurately by sceptics to be wholly subjective and barely convincing, yet nonetheless, the tales are served up for cognitive consumption to the palates of the gullible on a supportive plate of faith.

Imagining a first father god is a way of aspiring to a level of intelligence that humans do not have. The greater intelligence of a first father who knows how to make the environment and life, can also be implored to change conditions of the earth and human experience for the better. Relying on an imagined greater intelligence is better than relying on real lesser and limited human intelligence. Many individuals have little confidence and faith in their own intelligence to think and to comprehend. They are therefore vulnerable and easily fall victim to the artistically fabricated story of a monotheistic first father who will listen, think, comprehend, and act for them.

A first father god is a subjective idea that has gained credence over the years. Monotheistic authorities have encouraged faith and trust in what is a simple artistic word portrait of a first father. During times of crisis, clergy helpers reinforce the idea of a first father to be more real by displaying kindness, a caring attitude, and helpful assistance that represents the attitude of the imagined god.

The higher level of patience and kind assistance provided by clergy, convince individuals that they represent a first father god who has the same and an even higher and benevolent loving attitude toward humans. A first father god is a literary distraction from reality, an imaginal good portrayed with the use of words, and made apparent to comprehension as an abstract word portrait.

An imagined monotheistic intelligent first father is pragmatically utilized to transcend the non-intelligent semi-orderly environment, and the lower often disorderly intelligence of humans. Through monotheistic use of word art, the environment made by a first father, becomes vicariously subordinate to humans rather than what is observably true.

Human praise is reserved for the behavior of a first father ancestor rather than the behavior of the environment as the real origin and support of life. Paying attention to an artistic crafted word art of a first father god, Middle East, European, and Western cultures for quite some time now, have overlooked the direct and real continuation of human behavior with the behavior of the environment. The real forceful willing-like behavior of the environment, the energy elements of the earth and motion of the universe, are neglected in favor of an imagined artistic word story of a first father. The good and evil earth as origin is ignored and made subordinate to the exclusive good of a first father. Humans are direct descendants of a real, good and evil earth, and not the imagined word art of a good first father. Only in modern times have biochemists and physicists examined the lowly soil of the earth to therein find the hidden treasure of fine grain energy particles that function to animate and support biological life.

In monotheistic religions, the real animating energy of the soil is treated as unimportant dirt, and surpassed for a gaudy word portrait story of a first father god. For shame, to indulge in this separating sin and delusion which much of humankind unashamedly continues to accept.

With words, monotheistic leaders display the artistic portrait of a first father god beginning. Monotheistic religion seeks to convert individuals by utilizing the word art of story.

Monotheistic authors and authority figures utilize written and verbal instruction during religious services to make and exhibit the word portrait of a first father god so that the average person can behold and comprehend the beginning of existence. A first father god also serves to evoke filial piety and obedience to earthly fathers. Authority figures of monotheistic religions function as a stand-in for a first father god, and in so doing aspire to fatherly dominate a busy unthinking and immature population.

Aside from a small minority of hard core feministas, women are in the majority versus males when it comes to acceptance of a first father. Men utilize a first father god to dominate both men and women, and while women may realize this they use a first father to provide care and protection of the life they give birth to. For women, a first father justifies bringing forth of life and makes it worthwhile to risk the daily struggle of their children through accident, illness, ageing, dying, and death.

Monotheism is a lower form of religion as it is merely ancestor worship, a way of reconnecting with an artistically imagined first father. Worship of a male maker is also worship of human male traits that contribute to the female reproduction of life, and provide the superior male ability to make tools and weapons, and strength to provide food and protection for life to survive.

Communication

Many susceptible persons needing a response for assistance and answers to requests of prayer, have uncritically accepted the proffered word art of a first father god. Praying to a first father for an answer to a problem, is realistically to beseech the higher cerebral cortex of the brain. Alleged communications from a first father god to humans portrayed in the word stories of monotheistic scriptures are but expressions of creative artistic ability to identify an unknown beginning and as a way to obtain care and assistance.

A monotheistic first father god is not portrayed as an idol or work of art, as a visible image localized and limited in space and time.

A nonvisible first father god is not localized in space and time and is therefore not limited. A nonvisible god is alleged to be interactive with humans, not in appearance but as the inspiring cause of visions and dreams. An interactive god is but the innate ability of the cerebral cortex of the brain for dreams, intuition, psychic impressions, clairvoyant visions, and precognition.

Supposed communications from a first father god are the human brain's innate latent potential and overt expressed ability for extra-sensory perceptions. Unlike communications attributed to be from a first father god to special human prophets, anecdotal communications from an afterlife dimension to the living from deceased relatives are frequent and occur across a spectrum of society to many nonspecial and non-prophetical persons. Other exceptional experiences that occur to average individuals include anecdotal accounts of near-death experiences and childhood reincarnation memories. These experiences all relate not to a first father god but to another dimension and survival of an individual animating soul.

Helpless

The word portrait of a first father god is an artistic way of reducing human helplessness. All life forms are helpless at some time or other, helpless in an effort to acquire food and water, a sexual partner and to reproduce, and lack sufficient courage and aggression to survive. But only humans can imagine a first father god as an artistic way to reduce existential helplessness in knowing the beginning of existence.

Clever individuals insert themselves between the artistic imagined first father god and helpless individuals. Sacerdotalists realize the word portrait of a first father god readily appeals to many who are helpless, who need help in identifying where the environment and life comes from, need help with health, finances, relationships, and with general knowledge, and need ethical help in choosing right or wrong, good or evil.

Existential Relief

When ridden with existential angst in life, individuals search for relief. Many seek for someone or something to have confidence in, and to provide stability in the shifting sands of experience.

For monotheistic religions, the answer to the question of where to obtain relief from the stresses of life is to promote confidence in an imaginal first father, bolstered and supported with the word art of stories known as scripture. Confirmed in writing, the idea of a monotheistic god becomes more authoritative, palatable, and acceptable to many.

Humans find it difficult to be good and to refrain from the evil of excessive forceful willing. Monotheistic religions insist that without a first father who judges human behaviors and backs up his insistence on what is good by punishment, the quality of human life will be diminished. A first father god is but the imagined and enlarged version of the rudimentary version of a feeble human conscience.

The conscious and subconscious need for affection and protection of a biological father is projected and exploited by imagining the existence of a first father god who insists on obedience and cooperation among humans. These are real values of social authority projected onto the imagined patronage of a first father. The civilizing surface influence of an imagined external first father god is invoked to reduce the deeper and oftentimes ferocious internal demands of the animating soul for food and water, sex and reproduction, and aggression. The spontaneity of human behavior is animated by nonreasoning emotion and a triune soul.

If the origin of existence is accepted to be rational, though poignant human experience suggests otherwise, then life must also be rational. But this is a specious assumption. Human life is partially rational via the evolved cerebral cortex of the brain but is mostly incapable of reasoning and is irrational via the midbrain and body, the dynamic of which is an animating and willing soul of hunger for food and water, sex and reproduction, and aggression.

Disaster

The English word disaster (Latin dis, away from, plus astro, star) suggests that a person lacks or is away from a good or lucky star. The word suggests there is a lack of a lucky star, or a bad influence of stars, or some unknown negative force beyond the stars.

The origin of stars and earthly events is not an artistic word portrait of a benevolent monotheistic god but a cosmological force, of which atom and electron energy is a continuation, and of which the earth and life is a continuation. With this real pedigree, life is truly a disaster in the making.

With hunger for food and water, sex and reproduction, and aggression animating life, it is meant to be a disaster. Disasters there are many, including environmental events, accidents, physical and mental illness, divorce, suicide, crime, murder, war, a myriad of sufferings and sorrows, ageing, senility, and death. During the disaster of old age, gradually, one by one, chores, tasks, goals, and work are done with, and interests and relationships wane as energy for daily life subsides.

To counter this natural progression of minor and major disasters from the environment and daily life, some individuals imagine a first father god to exist. The artistic imaginal monotheistic god is clung to as an explanation for the beginning, to at least subjectively reduce the risks and disasters of living, and clung to as a comfort during an eventual slow dying or sudden death. For the average person, dying is frightening and is a final disaster, especially if conscious and alone. Even with friends and relatives present, there is only some small comfort and the dying person usually exhibits fear and anxiety about the final disaster of life, relinquishing possession of the body in death.

For a dying person, to no longer remain alive to be in the company of relatives and friends leaves a void. Most persons nearing death prefer some strong presence to be available to assist while encountering an unknown realm or possible oblivion. Hence, a first father is appealed to by many dying persons.

While comforting, the god of monotheistic religions is unfortunately a cognitive disaster, a subjective artistic imagining existing only in words of story, and does not exist as objectively real. While dying is uncomfortable and often a painful disaster for a brief or an extended time, at least one benefit of dying is that it is a way out of the burdens of living, with its many accidents, addictions, aggressions, depressions, disappointments, failures, illnesses, injuries, and relationships.

Astrology

Monotheistic religions trace human behavior and misbehavior to an artistically imagined first father god. The practice of astrology also leads to a misguided and retrograde comprehension of the origin of human behavior. Maybe ass-ology might be a better term for the practice of star gazing. Astrology is a superstitious attempt to relate human behavior with the gross behaviors of planets and arbitrary patterns of star constellations. Astrology is a crude metaphor that attempts to portray in a false way, the connection of the individual with real cosmological motion, and particles of energy as movement of atoms and electrons.

Astrologers chart the movements of stars and planets and offer advice individuals can follow. Crude astrology falsely claims that constellations of stars and planets shape the personality and influence the behaviors of humans. By asserting that star and planet behaviors determine human behaviors, astrology does not make use of a story first father figure.

Like monotheistic religions, astrology needs to look no further than within the human body to glimpse the causes of behavior, an animating soul that is a continuation of the behavior of earth, consisting of the behaviors of particle energy. Astrology needs to turn attention to marvel at the behavior of an observed relative and local motion of the universe ever moved by an unobserved nonlocal or omnipresent cosmological force.

Sexuality

For monotheistic religions, the human effort to make known the beginning of existence consists of referring to a past time along the line of human reproduction to artistically imagine a first father origin of the sequence. As a verbal and written work of art, the god artistically represents the biological beginning of existence. Psychologically, the god represents the human male cerebral cortex of the brain where the idea of a first father begins. The god also represents the physical reproductive male penis that contributes to life in the female womb. The first father of monotheism is a mental character, a literary totem by name only to represent the collective genital reproduction of the group.

Sexuality is important in monotheistic religions and the emphasis is appropriate as a first father god represents the sexual reproduction of the ethnic culture. The importance of sexuality is deserving of prominent mention in monotheistic writings. Examples include the biblical Garden of Eden story where the first two humans obtained the knowledge of nudity and sexual reproduction from the first father god's special tree. (Genesis 3:7,16; 4:1-2) The scriptures of the Islamic Quran allow a man to have a limit of four wives for his sexual pleasure. (Sura 4:3)

The monotheistic religion of Christianity displays a general antipathy toward sexual experience. Mary the mother of Jesus is portrayed by the Catholic church as not having sex with a human male, and she reproduced only through a sexual encounter with a first father god. A product of reproduction, the birth of the infant Jesus is celebrated by Christians. While keeping suspiciously close company with Mary Magdalene, Jesus is not mentioned in the four biblical gospels as having sex with a woman. Therefore, the Catholic sacraments require priests, who represent Jesus, to be celibate. Recognizing the importance of sexuality, the Christian religion directs attention away from its strong influence by artistically imagining and utilizing words to sketch the portrait of a supposed nonsexual, yet a human genital-making first father who impregnated a young virgin.

Celibacy

The gospels do not mention if Jesus did have or did not have sex, though there is mention of much time spent with Mary Magdalene. The practice of celibacy is on firmer ground with the artistic word art of monotheism. The unequaled first father god has no spouse to have sex with. Of course, based on alleged story events, (Luke 1:35) a young woman may just suffice.

There is no call for celibacy in either Judaism or Islam. Probably influenced by Hindu and Buddhist traditions, there is a monastic ascetic tradition of celibacy in Christianity. Monotheists may practice celibacy as a way of seeking visual or audible answers of comprehension from a first father god. Celibacy is a benefit as it does afford the luxury for training a focus of attention and reducing family and social distractions, and time is much better spent in meditative self and soul exploration.

Having a spouse, children, and an excess of family and friends are distracting as are routine chores of maintenance to home and vehicle, commuting, shopping, and socializing. The risks of celibacy are that it usually cannot be comfortably practiced. The strong forceful drive for sex can derange mental ability to focus attention. Irritability and conflict usually ensue, and neurotic symptoms often develop caused by sexual frustration.

The average conscious cerebral cortex of the brain fails to comprehend that it is the origin of any artistic imagined idea of a god. In praying to a first father, if an answer arrives to a problem, it originates from intuition or insight occurring in the brain. Prayerful seekers will only receive answers from their own brain, and failing that result, will receive mainly the less conscious and silent urges of hunger for food and water, sex, and aggression, the dynamic of an animating triune soul. Human experience consists of a mental and physical struggle between the idea of a first father located in the cerebral cortex of the brain, and the animating demands and willful urges located in the midbrain and body.

Celibacy as an emphasis occurs as a value of the cerebral cortex of the brain, precisely the location where a sexless good first father god is creatively and artistically imagined.

The higher cerebral cortex imagines a first father god as a pragmatic tool to exert moral and ethical control, and functions to direct attention away from lower desires and urges of the midbrain and body. The cerebral cortex brain functions contrast with the midbrain and body dynamic of a triune animating soul of hunger for food and water, sex and reproduction, and aggression.

Animating Soul

The cerebral cortex, alias the conscious self, seeks to solve the problems caused by the cerebellum, midbrain, and body, the dynamic function of which is the less conscious and subconscious animating triune soul. Imagining a first father is the artistic conscious effort to counter a real innate animating soul, the forceful demands of the body as hunger for food and water, sex and reproduction, and aggression.

The soul animates the physical body and yet unlike the body is metaphysical as its origin and roots are a continuation of energy particles of atoms and electron elements of the supportive earth. It is difficult to perceive and to know an animating soul, and to see how it is a continuation of the atom and electron energies of the environment. It is even more difficult to intuit all that moves to be a continuation and effect of a cosmological causal force. For the monotheistic masses, the metaphysical mechanism of reality must, of necessity be a simplistic spoon-fed pabulum knowledge of a first father god portrayed in the word art of story.

To solve the conundrum of how life was and is now animated, biblical word artists portray a fictional story of an authoritative god. The god stories of monotheism are subjective verbal works of art; the making of a word portrait and story images, and nothing more. The words of the biblical Genesis story, like pointer arrows, artistically turn attention in the direction of the beginning of existence to what is most easy to identify, a first father god.

The book of Genesis contains words accepted to be spoken by a first father god, yet the verbiage reflects only the limited knowledge of biblical word artist authors.

In monotheistic religions, the body must be resurrected by the first father as there is no inner animating soul. Not perceiving an animating soul, the biblical writers of Genesis could only imagine the animation of life to come from a first father. A monotheistic first father is imagined as a way of insuring that the body will be resurrected and will continue, and hopefully will not be punished, tortured, or destroyed by the god.

"In the sweat of thy face shalt thou eat bread, till thou return unto the ground; for out of it wast thou taken: for dust thou art, and unto dust shalt thou return." (Genesis 3:19)

In the twenty-first century, even usually reliable science lends support to the monotheistic view of a lack of evidence for an animating soul. In fact, the mundane word "self" has replaced the word soul in everyday language. A modern person has only a self, yet a lack of monotheistic or scientific evidence does not prevent popular faith and belief from accepting the existence of a human soul, and a general acceptance of it to be located somewhere inside the body, usually identified with conscious thinking ability.

A cosmological force that ever moves the universe is not human-like in any way. The imagining of a first father god, is the simple anthropomorphic way of identifying a cosmological force and particles of energy that animate life as a forcible willing triune soul of hunger for food and water, sex and reproduction, and aggression. As a continuation of force and energy, the soul animates and aids survival in life and post-death. The animating soul is a continuation of energy particles and a cosmological force, and is therefore resistant to destruction. The soul animates the physical body and unlike it, is metaphysical as its origin and roots are a continuation of energy particles and atom and electron elements of the supportive earth.

Speculating on what follows physical death, the energetic and forceful soul may exist as a dimensional phenomenon. A supernatural dimension is mostly conceived yet is also in some cases perceived. Anecdotal reports through the years include sightings of the deceased, childhood reincarnation memories, and near-death experiences.

These reports at least suggest alternative dimensions such as an afterlife may be just as real as an earthly dimension. In toto, these anecdotal and case study reports of existence after death suggest that other dimensions may well exist. Since the natural dimension of earth is real, there is also the possibility that other natural dimensions exist and adjoin it.

There is a probability that a willing pattern of behavioral energy developed in earthly life, may continue to resist destruction and to survive post-death in a way that words can only fall short and are unconvincing. Therefore, discussion about survival is moot, aside from anecdotal evidence. Suffice to say, as a continuation of force and energy from the environment, the animating of life by a triune soul of hunger for food and water, sex and reproduction, and aggression, assists life to survive and is resistant to destruction.

Dimensions

The first father god of Genesis made the earth, made the Garden of Eden, and then made the body of the first human from the earthly soil. First mention of an earthly underground cavern the god also made, called Sheol, is found in Genesis 37:35 when Jacob says, "For I will go down into the grave unto my son mourning." Early speculation was, when the body died, the shadow of the body survived and went to Sheol, a pit under the earth. The biblical first father of Genesis was preoccupied with and focused attention exclusively on the material earth and the human body made from it. Later there developed talk of resurrection and the belief that remains of the material body will be reanimated from the earth to live and breathe air again. Not until the time of the Israelite Jesus are immaterial afterlife dimensions mentioned.

A super first father god is the way the cerebral cortex of the brain artistically imagines and explains the origin of the super special planet earth and universe, and the super long line of ancestor sexual reproduction.

The story of a first father is an artistic word portrait and has nothing to do with a super nature, meaning dimensions of energy that transcend material dimensions. Any real dimensions that exist are super natures minus a first father god.

Limitless

For monotheistic religions, there is a terminus of the human body in a reward of an earthly paradise or a heaven, or in a burning fire of Gehenna or hell. If deserving, the one and only original physical body will be resurrected, a mere idea accepted and believed by many, and supported only by tradition.

In India, there is a process for an interminable continuation of many differing lives known as reincarnation. The Indian view is in accord with observation of energy particles of atoms and electrons and planets and galaxies, going around in circles. If observable reality is going in circles, may not the popularly speculated on unobserved reality of an animating soul do likewise?

Compared to the brief lifetime of humans, the observed motion of the vast universe seems like it will continue forever. Will the motion of the universe, ever cease? Not likely, as from a limited human perspective, the universe appears limitless and never ending. Since humans are the offspring of the limitless force and energy of the universe, it also seems unlikely the animating soul sprung from it will ever cease.

According to the accepted axiom of physics known as the theory of the conservation of energy, the usually unobserved circular quantum particles, atoms, and electrons of energy are not destroyed only transformed, to continue to seemingly exist forever. As a continuation of this forever process of energy, it may be inferred that the animating soul will continue to exist. Though it may also be inferred as well that through personal discipline, the triune force of the soul may be reduced and resolved. It is as a continuation of energy and cosmological force that confers resistance to destruction of an animating triune soul. A philosophical syllogism might be stated:

Force and energy are observed to be resistant to destruction;
The animating soul of life is a continuation of force and energy;
Therefore, the animating soul is resistant to destruction.

Life springs from the atom and electron energy elements of a material earth. The growth of plant and animal life is marked by an exuberance of animating force that moves the parts of life to grow and to coherently evolve. It is the cosmological force of universal motion and its seeds of quantum energy particles from which all of life goes and grows.

The seed, growth, and function of individual life is a forcible animating triune soul of effort as hunger for food, sex and reproduction, and aggression. The soul animates life and unlike the physical body is metaphysical as its origin and roots are a continuation of energy particles and atoms and electron elements of the supportive earth. The growing of life is relative to the going of energy particles and a greater moving cosmos. Without the going of energy elements, the growing of life would not exist.

As all plant seeds sprout from the soil, so do animal and human life sprout from and are supported by the ground of the earth. There is a known ground of atoms, electrons, and quantum particles of energy elements, and these are a continuation of an unknown ground of cosmological force that must, of necessity, be inferred from observation of the motion of the universe.

The primitive way of denoting a cosmic ground of force and energy, is to label it to be a monotheistic first father. The cosmic animating of relative going motion of the environment and growing of life, must for average comprehension be labeled as a god. Yet, one future day, the vague and obscuring fog of words that is monotheism will be lifted by the sunlit knowledge of the evolved wise offspring of the earth. The wise and mature sons and daughters of the earth will awaken to the objective fact that humans share a first father god that is only subjectively and artistically real.

It is not an empty sentiment to say that the real energy of the universe, earth and sun, is what is shared by all of life.

The relative motion that is time, takes care of all things and is what all is tied to, not an artistic imagined word portrait of a first father god but real particles of energy and a cosmological force.

A first father god is a hybrid concoction. An intelligent first father god primarily represents the conscious intelligence of the human cerebral cortex of the brain. As the imagined animator of life, the god is a substitute representation for an ignored but real animating triune soul of hunger for food and water, sex and reproduction, and aggression. The soul is a continuation of energy elements of the environment, and a cosmological force that exists on its own and ever continues to move the universe.

Fixating on an imagined first father god, biblical word artists failed to observe a real animating soul. A first father god as the animator of life is a substitute recognition for a non-recognized animating human soul. The soul is an animating function of sex and reproduction, of which hunger for food and water, and aggression round out a triad function. A triad is defined as:

"A group of three similar or closely related functions or things considered to be one unit having three parts."

The animating soul that forces life to exist and live, is a singular functional continuation of quantum particles, atoms, and electrons of energy elements, and a cosmological force of universal motion. As a continuation of energy, the animating and willing soul forces life to survive and live in three ways, as a willing triad or trio of hunger for food and water, sex and reproduction, and aggression.

Resistance to Destruction

Human life ends in the stillness and stiffness of rigor mortis. When body parts cease to function following the onset of death, that which animates it may not completely cease. Following death, the body is reduced to its constituent functioning smaller parts of energy particles, the momentum of which may be saved to continue in a coherent way.

The first theorem of thermodynamics or conservation of energy states that forms change and end but the energy of which it is composed is not destroyed. When the animating movement of the body ceases, the supportive energy particles within withdraw to coherently immerse in the safety of a greater dimension of quantum particles of energy and force.

The relative motion of the universe functions to continue, and in a sense, seeks to survive. The energy of the earth in a sense, seeks to maintain its material form and persist through changes conditioned by the surrounding environment. Cosmological force and the atom and electron energy elements of the earth and environment are resistant to destruction. The universe changes as relative motion and unseen energy maintains all relative forms. The living body changes but its animating essence as a continuation of cosmic and earthly force and energy is resistant to destruction. The body is physical while the soul animating it is metaphysical as its origin and roots are a continuation of energy particles and atoms and electron elements of the supportive earth.

Those unwilling to proceed through life on their own, prefer the artistically imagined word portrait of a first father god to accompany them. Monotheistic authorities and adherents imagine the visage of a first father to serve as a helper in life and to resist the personal destruction of death. However, a first father god is an imaginal and artistic construct of word art. The true resistance to destruction is internal, as a continuation of local external energy elements of the earth, and a cosmological nonlocal force that ever exists on its. The animating essence of humans is a continuation of the reality energy procession of the universe, and is therefore resistant to destruction.

Genes and chromosomes perform various functions within the varying cells and organs of living forms. These functions and behaviors are animated effects but are not the cause of the animating parts. The internal forceful function of animated behavior is a continuation of external particles of energy elements of the supportive earth. The internal animating of life is a forceful willing triune soul of hunger for food and water, sex and reproduction, and aggression.

Most of humankind fails to observe what it is that animates life. This cognitive failure has resulted in the origin and growth of monotheistic religions and the artistic belief of a first father god. If a first father neglects to save people living on earth from accidents and illnesses, it requires a huge leap of faith to accept the idea that a god exists to save humans in an afterlife.

Death

In a living cell, there is an effort to assemble and to function. The unobserved but felt effort in body cell and organ functions is a continuation of the energy particles of the environment. Effort of living cells cease when parts deteriorate, are injured or infected, and consequently fail to function. Effort desists and is gone, yet as a continuation of energy and force, the effort to live may coherently withdraw to another dimension. What holds life together continues to do so after death as there exists a seamless coherence of energy, effort, and force.

When the body ceases its willful movement, an animating soul may transit to another dimension. Supposed higher knowledge of a first father god is really experience of another dimension to which a willful human soul transits. To speculate, as mimics the neuroscience findings of biological life, the animating triune soul must also consist of mostly a less conscious and subconscious function of willing, and picture images consisting of ninety percent. This may be capped off with ten percent conscious remnants of willing and picture images of experience.

Sigmund Freud (1865-1939) in an essay written in 1915 (Thoughts for the Times on War and Death) observed that "…In the unconscious every one of us is convinced of his own immortality." Freud is correct but neglects to draw an accurate conclusion from his statement. Each is immortal as the subconscious function of the body, what Freud referred to as primitive biological instincts, is an ancient real animating triune soul that is resistant to destruction. The soul serves life to survive as an animating hunger for food and water, sex and reproduction, and aggression.

These forceful urges are a continuation of the energy particles and elements of the earth, and a cosmological force that ever exists on its own to move the ongoing universe.

When Sigmund Freud (1865-1939) the medical doctor made his theories of psychoanalysis known through lectures and publications, thousands of people attended his public forums and purchased and read his books. Professionals and laypersons alike realized Freud touched on some real intuitive truths about human experience. Based on his insightful investigation of mental hygiene, Freud wisely rejected his religious monotheistic heritage of a first father god.

However, so as to not be totally disobedient to the tradition of Judaism and thereby incur guilt, he did follow his religious-cultural tradition of only a biological reality of the body. Freud then viewed the animation of the body to consist of biological instincts, a container of a dynamic unconscious that he called the Id. His Jewish bias of not recognizing an animating soul in the Greek and Hindu tradition, led him to erroneous perception, comprehension, and conclusion.

The animating soul is a triune conscious and subconscious exertion of effort, a forceful hunger for food and water, sex and reproduction, and aggression. The origin of human willing effort is not an imaginal first father god but the real energy particles of elements and will-like behavior of a changing environment. The American poet Walt Whitman (1819-1892) whether based on sentiment or intuition, wrote:

"I do not dread the grave. There is many a time I could lay down and pass my immortal part through the valley of the shadow, as composedly as I quaff water after a tiresome walk. For what is there of terror in taking our rest?"

For Whitman, death should not be feared as the body reaches an inanimate condition while the animating soul continues in an ongoing journey of existence. How many can realistically see death in this way? The overwhelming majority fear the onset of old age and an approaching and inevitable, and often terrifying painful death.

Sensations of Death

Frightening experiences of life abound for humans, including injury, disease, ageing, dying, and death. There is a strong aversion and prohibition against seeing, smelling, and touching the dead body of an animal or human. Plants and trees not so much. Seeing a dead body, especially a human body in the various stages of rigor mortis, swollen, and decaying, has the immediate effect of revulsion and disgust.

The accompanying sensations of stench and decaying flesh of cells and organs is most hideous and appalling. In response to the two sensations of seeing and smelling of rotting and decaying flesh, there is a strong and immediate aversion and avoidance of nearing or touching the dead body. Touching the dead is avoided as fear of contagion must certainly be present as the need to avoid death spreading and happening to any individual nearing or touching the corpse. Sensations of hearing a dead person is less common unless the body emits noises of contraction and gurgling of fluids. The tasting of a dead body is usually not indulged in, unless the body is recently dead and fresh so that scavenging and cannibalism can occur on occasion.

Reincarnation

Not easy to exit through the birth canal and be born, and to get through daily living on the earth, and not easy dying and to depart from life. Life is a struggle with what exists on the inside of the body, and with what exists outside in the environment. Eventually through accident, illness, or ageing, the willful struggle of life is lessened and ends in death. The body no longer functions and can be observed to decay. When life is no longer animated, popular thought is that the conscious personality of the person leaves for an unknown dimension.

Yet the conscious self of wanting to be, do, or have is but the surface of the subconscious triune soul, the dynamic animating essence of life. The less conscious and subconscious background cellular function of the body, is the dynamic of an animating willing soul of hunger for food and water, sex and reproduction, and aggression.

Most humans run to and fro through life caring little to examine functions of their own brain and body.

Conscious attention is usually distracted by changing sensations and picture images of the brain. Attention is not stilled sufficiently to glimpse and to comprehend what if anything in the body is resistant to destruction. Therefore, it is not easy to sort out the functions of the conscious self and the subconscious strands of the soul, a singular continuation of force and energy having a triune function to enable survival.

Just as clothes, car, cell phone, computer, and relationships wear out, and by human willing intention are replaced by a new one, so is the human body worn out and a new body intended and willed to be acquired by an individual. This may not occur consciously but as a subconscious forceful willing urge to continue as the dynamic of an animating triune soul that is resistant to destruction. Less conscious and subconscious willing of life proceeds below the limen of conscious attention, and cares only for individual survival as a dynamic forcible animating hunger for food and water, sex and reproduction, and aggression. What matters most in life is to exist, to go on living and not to die or cease. The triune soul exists, and resistant to destruction can therefore re-exist. It is not any more amazing and a wonder to exist once; than it is to re-exist.

Archaeologists explore and locate skeletal remains of early humans, and their shelters and artifacts concealed in the soil of the earth. Like the work of archeologists, those dedicated to meditation explore and search out the remnants of an animating soul that may continue to linger as coherent memories of human willing preserved as a continuation in a background dimension of atoms and electrons of energy elements, and the generating field of a cosmological force that ever exists on its own.

The animating soul of life is a continuation of the supportive material earth that in turn is a continuation of a ground of supportive atoms and electrons elements of energy. The soul animates the physical body and yet is metaphysical as its origin and roots are a continuation of energy particles and atoms and electron elements of the supportive earth.

For a cycle of reincarnation to exist it must be dependent upon the earth dimension, human sexual reproduction, an alternative dimension, and a destruction resistant soul. No first father god is needed or necessary, and no first father helper exists either on the dimension of earth or in an afterlife dimension. A first father god is a artistic literary myth, while anecdotal and case study evidence suggests an afterlife dimension is real.

The activation of life is not a first father animator located outside of the body. Supported by the earth, animation occurs inside as an animating soul, a forceful willing hunger for food and water, sex and reproduction, and aggression. The animating soul is a direct continuation of the energy of the supportive earth. An animating soul resistant to destruction conducts each individual transition and journey as a continuation of particle energy and force. The universe is moved by a cosmological force. The changing motion of the environment consists of energy particles. What animates life must be a continuation of this cause and effect process. From an unformed cosmological field or ground, come particles of energy that form the environment, to then form the earth and form, support, and evolve life.

Being a continuation of a cosmological force that moves the universe, and being a continuation of atoms and electron energy, is what confers the resistance to destruction of an animating triune soul. A cosmological force generates the environment, and the energy particles of the earth generate, support, and animate and evolve life. The animating soul functions on its own as a continuation of the environment composed of the energy of quantum particles, atoms, and electrons, and as a continuation of a cosmological force that ever moves the universe.

The environment of galactic motion of the universe appears to survive a long and probably infinite time. Human willing effort is a continuation of this cosmological force and energy of the universe. As observed by astronomers and cosmologists, the effort of the universe is to expand while the reality of its particle motion is to go in circles. The universe consists of forces such as gravity and magnetism and quantum energy particles of atoms and electrons that are resistant to destruction. Life is a continuation of this animating process.

Human willing function of body and brain is limited. The only true strength of human willing is its resistance to destruction, a trait of the animating soul conferred upon it not by a first father god but by where it has originated from. The environmentally generated and evolved cerebral cortex of the human brain generates the artistic idea and story of a first father god.

In monotheistic religions, the conscious cerebral cortex deifies its own function by artistically imagining a knowing intelligent first father god that is the causal agent of the environment and life. A monotheistic first father god is an imagined helper and savior while the only real help to live and survive is an animating triune soul that contributes to individual survival.

In monotheistic story, the origin of existence is completely outside of humans and is identified to be a first father god. A first father is an imagined mechanism to explain the animation of life that originates from and is supported by a real environment. The force of universal motion and elements of energy particles are continued inside of life as an animating triune soul, a dynamic willing hunger for food and water, sex and reproduction, and aggression.

Forces of magnetism and gravity, and energy particles, are observed to be long lasting. If anything survives death of the human body, the mechanism must be related to force and energy. The living body has an origin in the quantum particles, atoms, and electrons of the elements of the environment that originate and support life. Therefore, by necessity, the animating soul of life is long lasting and resistant to destruction.

The long-lasting and resistant to destruction qualitative function of an animating soul is a continuation of relative energy and cosmological motion of the universe. As observed, the motion of the universe continues every instant, and particles of energy are transformed but are resistant to destruction.

Hunger, sex, and aggression are not just physiological body urges, they are a triune soul function derived from particles of energy that are a continuation of the environment. The life urge and effort to move and survive, comes from and is a continuation of metaphysical energy particles of the earth, and is therefore resistant to destruction. This is the animating willing soul of life that comes from a cosmological Go and not from a God.

While often considered bad and evil from a cerebral cortex point of view, the trio of dynamic soul traits are a continuation of metaphysical particles of quantum, atom, and electron energy, intuited and inferred to be a continuation of a cosmological force. The subconscious willing of the animating soul functions to survive and continue. Subconscious willing of the body functions with a minimum of supervision and interference by conscious attention and willing. At the cellular level, subconscious willing wants food and water, sex and reproduction, and aggression.

Conscious attention, picture images, and willing manage well or badly to direct the subconscious triune forces of the animating soul to obtain satisfaction. Subconscious cellular willing functions demand that conscious willing do much of what it wants. Otherwise, subconscious willing can wreak havoc for conscious attention and willing by causing symptoms of mental discomfort and somatic dysfunctions.

Through moderate discipline and training, it is possible to moderate the triune force of hunger, sex, and aggression. Intuitively, the animating force of the soul can be disciplined and guided to go in a better or worse direction, and can only be gradually reduced from existing. Without observation and examination, comprehension, and discipline, willing ever continues. Curbing willfulness by moderate ascetic disciplines is a way of reducing the influence of the internal animating soul, to guide it to a gradual stop.

In contrast, monotheism fails to recognize the existence of an internal animating soul, and seeks to reduce and limit the evils of life only by directing attention externally to an imagined first father god.

Generally, humans have a strong desire not to perish and to continue to exist. The ground of the universe may just grant the human desire to continue. A few may want to perish into oblivion from the troubles and burdens of life. Willing not to exist by destroying the body does not destroy the animating soul. Dimensions may exist to readily accommodate a soul that is resistant to destruction as a pattern of conscious and subconscious habitual willing that wants to continue to exist. A natural dimension existing beyond the earth is randomly glimpsed and reported by some who have had a near-death experience and had contact with the deceased or ghosts.

Most individuals want to continue to exist at any cost, either in life or an afterlife. They would be better served to instead desist from wanting to exist. It is not easy to desist or to de-exist, and is impossible for most as very few investigate what animates life and even fewer are up to the task of disciplining, directing, and reducing the forceful animating soul. To be free of that which causes life and is also resistant to destruction is difficult.

Force and energy are the substrate of the soul that on the earth objectifies a living body. As a continuation of the environment, the soul forms, animates, and breathes the body to live and survive, beats the heart, obtains, digests, and expels food, and forcefully insists on sex and reproduction. Human life is a continuation of energy and force within the body that continues by default. The animating soul within is a continuum of the energy of the earth and cosmological motion of the universe. Human willing to exist is a continuation of energy and force, and therefore resistant to destruction has a potential to re-exist.

Motion Sickness

The cosmological motion of the universe continues seemingly unceasingly, and just as the earth composed of circular energy elements continues to rotate and revolve endlessly, so too as a continuation of this does an animating soul continue.

There is no real need of a first father to save an individual. At some level of depth in awareness and comprehension, each realizes the animating soul of life and its resistance to destruction.

Nearing death, there should be a quiet assurance of continuation of willing to exist. There is a continuance unless interest has developed in life to reduce and to guide willing to a state of saintly ceasing.

Glimpsing the endless abyss of existence, some seek to lessen the often-nauseous inducing journey of life, and console themselves with an offered first father god of monotheistic religions. Some few look to wake from the nightmares of life by seeking knowledge to better comprehend it. Others may seek to obtain money to make life more tolerable and comfortable. Then too, some take desperate measures to lessen the induced motion sickness on the endless journey and struggle that is life, by taking the situation into their own hands and ending it.

Apperception

What animates life, a first father god, or the environment and an animating soul? A first father is an imagined artistic word portrait. Worship of a first father god accomplishes three things. An intelligent first father explains where the environment and life come from, affirms the biological reproduction of ancestors, and emphasizes the superiority of the cerebral cortex of the brain that imagines a human-like beginning.

The animating factor of life is a real supportive earth and a triune soul. n conscious attention of the cerebral cortex of the brain, hunger appears willed by the less conscious and subconscious force to find food and water, sex and reproduction, and aggression, as a triad soul function of an animating force. In monotheistic religions, the animating force inside the body, is erroneously conceived by the cerebral cortex of the brain to be a first father animator projected to the outside of the body. An imagined first father god figure is an applique that cloaks and conceals a real animating soul that is a continuation from and is supported by the earth, and is an extension from a cosmological force that moves the greater universe.

The cognitive error of a first father can be resolved by an apperception that the cerebral cortex of the brain is the conceiver and projector of a god figure. In this way, the monotheistic conceived split and separation of humans from their origin is resolved. The resolution of biblical separating sin, is accomplished only on the inside by an ascendency of apperception and comprehension occurring in the cerebral cortex, that the midbrain and body dynamic is an animating triune soul of hunger for food and water, sex and reproduction, and aggression. The cognitive process of perception is defined as:

"The detecting and interpreting of sensations from the environment through sensory receptors, a cognitive determination by the brain of what exists and a resulting behavioral response."

In contrast, apperception is a continuation of the perceptual process and is defined as:

"To consciously perceive that one is perceiving. To comprehend an immediate perception, and to assimilate and relate it to previous perceptions and conceptions formed in the brain."

Apperception is the ability to observe at least some perceptions as they form in conscious attention. The process of apperception is how invention, insight, and intuitive and psychic impressions originate. For the average person, the ability of holding conscious attention still, for the purpose of observation, is not developed, and the ability for perception and apperception is limited. Attention is easily distracted by sensations, picture images of past and future, and associations.

Ability for apperception of what occurs in the cerebral cortex of the brain, and midbrain and body functions, must be developed. The cerebral cortex of the brain subjectively imagines a first father god that is popularly accepted to exist objectively. However, the notion of a first father can be apperceived to be located exclusively in the subjective artistic imagining of the conscious cerebral cortex of the brain.

Apperception must also occur of the animating soul to be a less conscious and subconscious dynamic force of hunger for food and water, sex and reproduction, and aggression. Once apperceived as such, the triune force can be better trained so as not to overly interfere with a focus of conscious attention and concentration.

Conscious willing effort strains for pleasures and against pains, and is of necessity bonded with, and part and parcel of sensations of the senses, and resulting picture images of now, past, and future. Meditative observation sorts through and investigates conscious and less conscious picture images, and less conscious and subconscious willing behaviors of brain and body functions. Meditative attention and observation calms effervescent sensations of the senses, calms the second by second change of conscious picture images, and brings the ever-straining conscious mental willing to moments of rest. Perceptual clarity and intuitive comprehension is the beneficial result.

Self and Soul

To learn and to comprehend life and the environment is the best of human accomplishments. Unfortunately, only a minority are serious about learning, and even fewer seek knowledge of the self and soul. There are continuing and repetitive distractions of life that require attention, such as relationships, finances, health, ageing, and traditions that usually interfere with and distract from better comprehension. The young study language, math, and science, and yet no skills are taught of how to observe and comprehend the conscious self and the less conscious and subconscious soul functions.

What is referred to as the human self consists of conscious attention, picture images, reasoning, willing behavior, and personality. Recognition and respect is directed mainly to the conscious self of the cerebral cortex of the brain as the reasoner, investigator and inventor of tools and weapons. Yet the cerebral cortex is not apperceived and appreciated to be the artistic imaginal maker of a monotheistic first father god.

Lack of recognition and therefore little respect is directed to the less conscious and subconscious animating triune soul of life.

What is referred to as the human soul, has traditionally meant a presence in the human body that survives physical death. However, only vague definitions of what the soul consists has been offered. Naïve and popular writings abound on the topic of the human soul, including New Age riff of a good and special soul, and for some Christian groups, an animating spirit or breath worth saving, and reattaching it to a resurrected body by a first father god.

The only appropriate broad definition of the soul is that it is what animates life. The soul is a dynamic trinity, a triune force of life and is not related to an artistically imagined monotheistic word portrait of a first father god. What is real are earthly efforts for food and water, sex and reproduction, and aggression as the primal willing forces for survival. The soul dynamic is expressed as three main systems of the physical body:

Digestion and circulation of food and water
Genitals and reproduction organs
Smooth and striated muscles for aggression

These systems are the essence, the essentials of life, and the individual is forcefully aroused by them to willing act as the dynamic behaviors of an animating triune soul of hunger for food and water, sex and reproduction, and aggression. The conscious cerebral cortex of the brain oversees, judges, and attempts to direct these powerful midbrain and body systems, with partial success. The evolved cerebral cortex of the brain can only sort through and attempt to direct the arousing, exciting, and often disturbing and agitating less conscious and subconscious miasma of the triune soul.

Few seek to observe and to better comprehend the conscious self and the subconscious soul of life. In popular thinking, to be selfless is good but to say someone is soulless is bad. How so? The conscious self is primarily the cerebral cortex, and the midbrain and body functions are the subconscious soul, a triune animating essence and essential force of life. To be soulless is to not recognize a kinship of a shared an animating and willing essence.

There is blame for the conscious self for its poor judgements, uncritical knowledge, and rash behaviors but it is the triune soul as the animating subconscious essence of life that is more deserving of blame.

It is not easy to focus conscious attention and to observe functions of the self, such as perception, conception, picture images of past and future, and willing. There are continual internal and external distractions of living. Attention is conditioned and mostly limited to daily personal survival and to what is familiar and habitual. Daily tasks such as work and relationships demand much attention. When tiredness arrives, little attention is directed to the dynamic of sleep and dreams.

External sensations stimulate and demand internal attentiveness, as do picture images of memory and future events that distract conscious attention. The individual is aroused to act on the inside of the body by the powerful animating soul that forcefully directs conscious attention to body functions and stimulates behavior of willing effort and determination to acquire what is needed.

An animating triune soul subconsciously wills hunger for food and water, sex and reproduction, and aggression, and relevant picture images are reflected in conscious attention. The triune soul forces the body to move and behave and forces the cerebral cortex of the brain to make picture images of how best to proceed. Hunger demands that attention and behaviors be directed to obtaining food and water. Sex demands that attention and behaviors be directed to obtaining a lover or spouse. Aggression directs words and behaviors to a target.

Comprehension

Life is the dual effort to find what is good and to avoid the potential of painful struggle and inevitable evils. Some impaired humans attempt to separate themselves from encounters with earthly evils by artistically imagining a good first father god. The good of a first father is only subjectively imagined.

The real and the good of existence is to be traced to reducing participation in the mixed good and evil of existence by reserving time to observe what truly animates life internally. To seek what is good in life is to find and to comprehend what animates it, and to reduce and moderate its animating force.

In the monotheistic religions, the human soul has been missing for quite some time now. For monotheism, the soul has not been recognized to exist. Its concealed presence is detected in the long vaunted theological insistence that humans have been endowed with a free will by their first father god. However, the free will seems to be considered mortal along with the physical body. Only the immortal free will of the first father can reanimate the free will and body of a deceased person during a future group resurrection.

The only real powerful willing is not outside of humans but within them as an animating soul that is resistant to destruction following physical death of the body. A real human free will opposes death by being a continuation of energy particles. Humans subjectively seek to oppose death by imagining the powerful will of a first father god who made life and can also remake it. A willing first father is only imagined but a real human free will is resistant to destruction.

Human free will is a continuation of the willing-like change of the real environment composed of energy particles. The human body is formed from the earth but the real former and animator, is not an external first father but an internal animating soul that is a continuation of the supportive energy particles of the earth. The soul is a dynamic of hunger for food and water, sex and reproduction, and aggression.

As a continuation of energy, no individual can destroy or escape the animating and less conscious and subconscious willing soul; it can only be resolved. Some destroy their body as a way of seeking relief from life in a supposed oblivion but the animating essence continues to exist. Many foolishly seek help in dealing with and directing the real animating soul by imagining and appealing to a first father god.

An imaginal external first father god fortifies individual internal willing to be strong and to survive the evil onslaughts of existence that sooner or later result in the slaughter of individual life through accident, aggression, ageing, and death.

Pleasures

People known, things possessed, and places inhabited, are usually pleasurable but also can soon become routine and inflict the pain of boredom. Therefore, humans like to take trips or buy new things. New people, places, and things relieve the tediousness and wearisome dull pain of boredom. Just as an individual who runs down a steep hill has to continue running and not stop too abruptly as to do so they would lose balance and fall, in a similar way, each person in life continues to run from pleasure to pleasure. An individual who attempts to stop too abruptly or for a prolonged time, risks losing balance by falling into the tedious pain of boredom.

Unfortunately, during the continuing necessity of walking or running from pleasure to pleasure, the individual is sure to encounter unexpected and unbalancing experiences of disappointment, accident, illness, loss, and various verbal and physical aggressions of the day. Small sequential pleasures serve to keep an individual moving forward in life to reduce the onset of existential angst and despair.

Smile

For most humans, the goal of life is to go from pleasure to pleasure and to avoid pains. A smile generally communicates to observers that the smiling person is experiencing a state of pleasure or is at least free from pain. With a display of cheerful smiles, monotheists like to show to others how uplifted they are. The often pathetic display of superficial happiness comes not from without but from within when the subjective idea of a first father god is accepted to exist externally. Monotheists like to display cheerful and often smug and superior smiles of happiness and charity as they imagine they are favored by a first father, and will obtain approval and acceptance from the god.

Monotheists also smile as they have a helper who will one day resurrect their physical body so they will continue to exist, and will inhabit their same bodies again.

Contrast the deluded smiles of monotheistic adherents, with the smile of happiness portrayed on sculptures of the Buddha (circa 623-543 BCE). The slight smile of the Buddha denotes the happiness of the animating soul calmed in its restless quest to obtain food, have sex and reproduce, and to express aggression.

Group Think

Research evidence suggests that it is innate with individuals to seek to conform with group values and norms. Doing so promotes agreement, comfort, and cooperation among members, and in turn contributes to individual and group survival. Individuals cooperate with others to better obtain food, have sex and reproduce, to increase aggression, and to generally survive. The term groupthink is generally defined as:

"A psychological dynamic in which individuals of a group seek to reduce controversy and conflict among members, and to reach agreement and consensus by avoiding investigation of and by suppressing dissenting viewpoints."

Critical discussion is discouraged and lack of criticism promotes conformity and harmony. The result is often an impaired ability to think rationally about a topic or other realistic alternative choices. The group may further defend its viewpoints by separating themselves from criticism of outside influences and by suppressing other or differing views. The ingroup overrates its held views to be superior, true and right, and denigrates the views of other outgroups as inferior, false, and wrong.

Monotheistic religions are prime examples of groupthink. To fit into a group that follows a loving and yet also punishing first father god is irresistible for many people. An imagined supportive strong first father, and real supportive group members, provide the benefit of mutual support. Therefore, all is well in the groupthink land of monotheism.

Investigation

All gods are objectively false as they are merely subjective artistic metaphors and reifications of real processes. Monotheistic authors shape their first father, not with stone, metal, or paints but with the artistry of words and story. The unverifiable idea of a first father is more permanent than a material sculpted or painted likeness. Introjected, accepted uncritically, and not investigated, the mere story idea of a first father god is promoted and passed from person to person and from generation to generation.

Acceptance of the mere idea of a first father god is promoted. There is no promotion of observation and methods to investigate the idea of a first father god, only faith and belief are encouraged and promoted. Fixing attention on an imaginal first father ancestor located externally is offered rather than internal observation and investigation of self and soul.

None of the monotheistic religions, and only some of the Hindu yoga practices investigate the brain and body. The philosophies of Taoism, Heraclitus, and Arthur Schopenhauer also investigate existence. Buddhism is an early yet amazing depth psychology that teaches training to focus attention, to meditate and thereby declutter brain contents of excess picture images. In this way an individual can reach unbiased and true perceptions and apperceptions.

Buddha (circa 623-543 BCE) advocated a consistent psychological practice of exploring brain and body processes and functions. Buddha even forbade artistic images of his likeness to be made. He rightly emphasized meditative methods of self and soul exploration. Many average individuals find it difficult to look within and to observe brain and body processes. For Buddha, the best way to live is to avoid the many distractions of life by retreating to the forest and there to train attention not on art images and word stories of gods but to stillness and so to better observe, investigate, and learn about real brain and body functions.

Group Care

Consorting with a crowd is a group effort of willing for similar and shared results. In contrast, it is an individual effort to focus and steady attention for the purpose of better comprehending brain and body functions. It is an individual effort to guide willing and to accept good and bad outcomes. It must be an individual effort to reduce and moderate the animating triune soul of hunger for food, sex and reproduction, and aggression.

Knowledge benefits, refines, and directs willing. Willing is not a reasoning process but is a notorious unreasoning and animating of behavior, a doing or not doing process. Willing can be better managed by an adequate knowledge level that assists better results. Lacking knowledge, limits willing to the basic care of life, eating food and drinking water, sex and reproduction, and aggression.

Ignoring and not observing how conscious and subconscious willing enables the individual to survive, many accept the proffered artistic imagined word portrait story of a caring first father. The weak vulnerable human ego finds it easy to imagine the strong ego and of a first father god who can provide care and assistance to survive.

Those who accept the idea of a first father group together, and thereby furnish support and care for each other. Humans seek care yet many often find it difficult to care for themselves in life and to obtain care from others. Finding meager care during life, the monotheistic answer to the problem of obtaining care is to imagine that a first father exists who cared enough to make the environment and life, and continues to care for humans today. The subjective mental construction of a caring first father god has long been portrayed in the monotheistic word portraits of scriptural stories.

Conflict

In the Genesis story, the first humans are portrayed in conflict with the first father god. Biblical writers were surely inspired to place conflict in the Genesis story as a way of explaining how humans are separate from a good life.

The story of the first father and the first humans, reflect the truth of the ever occurring and long-lasting behavior patterns of historical conflict that have and will always continue into the foreseeable future to plague humankind.

A first father imagined in story has a basis in and is supported by experience of real biological fathers. Rather than reporting on facts, biblical authors were surely inspired by observing humans to be in conflict, not only with biological fathers but with mothers, siblings, and with fellow humans in general. To have a biological father, and to conflict with him, is a somewhat painful emotional experience. The dynamic of a real biological model was taken and applied to a Genesis story disagreement with an imagined first father god, and later branded by Christian theologians as the fault and sinful separation of humankind. The first father punished the first two humans with a string of curses that Christian theologians insist, were later inherited by all human descendants as Original Sin. The many human guilts and separating sins of life come not from the opening of an imaginal first father's cursing mouth but from the real opening of the biological male penis and its discharge of sperm into the fertile female vagina to result in the pregnancy and birth of an infant.

Both genders are animated not by a first father god but by an often conflicting, demanding, and forcible triune soul of hunger for food and water, sex and reproduction, and aggression. One of the most intense pleasures of life is sexual orgasm, which, in part, is what the first father god of monotheism represents.

Monotheism is simply based on many previous sexually reproductive forefathers, psychologically compressed into one symbolic story summation of a nonsexual first father god. A first father god is artistic word art, portrayed in story and elaborated on as a way of explaining the beginning of the environment and life. Therefore, no objective evidence is insisted upon in monotheistic religions. Only subjective faith or trust is required as the first father exists only as an idea in the cerebral cortex of the brain.

The imagined willing of a monotheistic god, occurs only as a real conscious willing of the cerebral cortex of the human brain as an effort to explain its origin by imagining the story of a first father beginning. A first father god is carried around in the head of the monotheistic oriented person as a subjective idea conceived to be beneficial and protective. The idea is only subjectively real, and is supported only by flimsy faith and a false trust and subjective sense of security.

The biblical Genesis story of imagined conflict between a first father and the first humans, represents a real conflict between the conscious cerebral cortex, and the midbrain and body. The less conscious and subconscious midbrain and body dynamic is the animating triune soul of hunger for food and water, sex and reproduction, and aggression.

Addictions

Seeking artificial pleasures is a way of evading and reducing the pains of living. Many ingest temporary pleasures such as drugs, alcohol, and foods. Addictions to drugs, foods, sex, persons, and possessions, like habits, are difficult to remove. Indulging an addiction brings only temporary pleasure and relief from the pains of life.

Through hearing and reading, members of monotheistic religions introject and become addicted to the imagined artistic word portrait of a first father god. The many adherents of monotheistic religions are cognitively addicted to artistic word art as a way of knowing an unknown beginning of existence. Monotheism is an addiction to the ideational pleasure of a first father god and the imagined provided care and protection during life and death. A first father god is an artistic artifice, an imagining and making known with words only, the beginning of existence, and a making known of care and protection. An artistically imagined first father is a way of locating a human-like cause of the forms and functions of the environment and life. The god is a protective imaginal idea in response to the experience of human uncertainty of living, and the exiting change from the dimension of life to death.

Tangle

Daily life is a continual change of conscious sensations, picture images of the brain, and conscious and subconscious functions of body and behaviors. The individual human personality is a tangled web of conscious and subconscious willing functions difficult for the average person to comprehend and to control for the better. Monotheistic religions imagine a first father god as a cognitive tool who will assist humans by comprehending and controlling life and death for them.

Utilizing the biological cerebral cortex of the brain, monotheistic authors inspirationally and artistically imagine a story, a word portrait to explain the origin and function of the environment and human behavior. For the early Semitic brain, the need and drive to know the origin and function of the environment and life resulted in the poorly contrived artistic product of story, a word portrait of a first father god. The portrait of the god is hung in the firmament of imagination as a way of identifying the beginning of existence, and as a way of seeking what is good and caring in an often bad and uncaring earthly existence. Attention to the imagined story of a first father god obscures the origin from and plain dependence of life on the environment.

A monotheistic god is a perspective that overlooks the earth as the real origin of life. Instead, the purveyors of a first father direct attention to an imagined god. A first father who is imagined and portrayed as making a good beginning, is a utilitarian way of taking attention away from the plethora of both good and evil real earthly experiences.

The behavior of a jealous, caring, and protective god (Exodus 34:14) is an artistic way of overriding the risks, evils, and potentially deadly behaviors of the environment and fellow humans. An imagined rational eternally stable first father is much more preferred over a real non-rational and unstable changing environment, and a limited semi-rational and partially stable conscious human self, and an irrational subconscious animating triune soul. Having a first father, human reason can then appeal to a greater reason to make life a reasonably better experience. A first father god is not the most reasonable and scientific explanation of the beginning but is the most imaginative and artistic.

Monotheism deludes human reason with an artistic story that advocates faith and trust in a greater imagined reason, the ultra-reasoning of a first father god with knowledge of how to make the environment and life. Human reason is limited to what it can observe and measure but humans can compensate for their limitations by imagining stories of a first father that has unlimited reasoning ability. Imagining a first father god is a way of going beyond limited human reasoning to a greater reasoning. Human life is animated not by an external super reason but by an internal unreasoning animating triune soul that is a continuation of a semi-orderly and nonreasoning environment.

Waste of Time

The only true way to remove the separating sin of humans from their shared origin, is to cease to imagine it to be a first father, and to accept that the god exists only subjectively as an artistic imaginal story. 6What a waste of time, looking for a first father god. Searching for a first father, an individual must not look for an external presence but must look closer at the internal cerebral cortex of the brain that subjectively imagines the god to exist objectively.

It is truly a waste of time to search for a first father god anywhere else than as an ideational image in the cerebral cortex of the brain. What a waste of time to read monotheistic scriptures as the writings are only and exclusively subjective artistic word portraits of a first father god made by the human cerebral cortex of the brain. Monotheistic writings are a subjective artistic "his story" orientation that emphasize the importance of male lineage. The stories of a monotheistic god are subjective word art and are not objective history. Even actual historical events are subjectively interpreted and not objective.

In the search for a first father, internal attention is directed to an external fatherly god for help. Yet it is obvious to apperception that it is the higher cerebral cortex of the brain that imagines and makes up word story portraits about a parental god. Individuals who retreat to a monotheistic seminary do so with the intention to search for and to find evidence for the existence of a first father god.

What a waste of time spent in seminarian study and search for a first father. A monotheistic god is a mere literary word portrait of a human-like beginning.

As a monastic or seminary resident, an individual may conduct a contemplative and prayerful search to find and comprehend what animates life. Attention eventually becomes bored with attempting to find an objective first father when realistically the imagined idea exists only subjectively. Attention also soon becomes quite fatigued with any efforts to meditatively observe and comprehend an internal spirit or breath of life. Both searches are fruitless efforts as a first father and the internal spirit of life will not be found.

In the biblical Genesis story, the soul is wrongly conceived to not exist, and life is imagined to be animated by a first father who breathed life into the first humans and later cursed and separated himself from them. In the Genesis story, the first two humans were not made with a soul but were only made to breathe (Hebrew ruah) and to live as a living (Hebrew nephesh) body. There is no Hebrew or Jewish word for soul, such as the Greek word *psyche* or the Hindu word *atma*. Therefore, in the Genesis story there is no animating soul to account for human behavior, (Genesis 3:19) only a life. (Genesis 2:7)

Rules

In both Eastern and Western monastic traditions, there are salient and striking rules in three main areas of human behaviors. There are rules of restrictions on eating times and amounts and kinds of food, no sex and reproduction, and the rule of reducing aggression by developing contemplation on and behaviors of compassion, love, and forgiveness.

The restricting rules on these specific behaviors are a way the cerebral cortex of the brain seeks to remedy, correct, and direct the midbrain and body functions of an innate animating and willing soul. The animating soul is a willful dynamic of hunger for food, sex and reproduction, and aggression. The ruling force of these three deep-seated essential behaviors, is such that conscious reasoning of the cerebral cortex of the brain finds them difficult to control.

Seminary and monastic rules function to reduce and make less forceful what is conceived by monotheistic religions to be humankind's sinful and accursed condition. More to the truth, the internal struggle is between the higher cerebral cortex that imagines a first father god, and the lower dynamic of midbrain and body as a real animating triune soul of a forcible willing hunger for food and water, sex and reproduction, and aggression.

Assistance is rendered to those who struggle with the essence of life by imagining the existence of a first father, who is also a god. In this way, imagined external help is rendered for an internal deficit of personal ability for insight and knowledge.

Seek and Find

Rather than focusing on a first father god, a seeker looking for what animates life must instead observe the internal willing force of hunger for food, sex and reproduction, and aggression, and with a focus of attention willfully exert effort and discipline to moderate and make the soul less forceful. The triune soul is the forceful will to live that is resistant to destruction and that can only be lessened by observation, training, and discipline. The compulsive trouble-making less conscious and subconscious dynamic of the soul, assails and hijacks a conscious focus of attention. The conscious cerebral cortex is often assailed by the less conscious and subconscious midbrain and body, and its dynamic demands of hunger for food and water, sex and reproduction, and aggression. If knowledge of the soul is lacking, the cerebral cortex of the brain usually resorts to imagining a first father god for assistance.

The conscious cerebral cortex of the brain is also assailed by its own ability to make picture images. To get closer to a first father god is a metaphor for having a higher or improved clarity of the cerebral cortex of the brain. Lack of a focus of attention clouds the cerebral cortex with its own excess images of past memory and future imaginations. A stream of superficial picture image distractions, limiting associations, and habits prevail.

To get closer to a first father god is to both reduce the internal compulsions of the triune soul, and to reduce excess picture images of future events and past events as memory, so that intuitive clarity of perception can develop. If the animating triune soul dominates, and an excess of picture images prevail, the higher god-like abilities of the cerebral cortex of the brain, such as apperception, extra-sensory perception, and creative invention are obscured.

The conscious cerebral cortex is conditioned to produce copious picture images that in popular vernacular are called thoughts or thinking. What is called thought, is a conscious or subconscious picture image of an object appearing in a spacetime sequence. A thought is attention directed to an object in spacetime, as an indistinct or distinct image. Excess distracting conscious picture images are lessened through a practice of focusing attention and meditation.

Then conscious attention may reside in clarity, poise, and peace. Disciplined meditative states of conscious attention, focus to reduce sensations and picture images of the cerebral cortex of the brain. There is a calming of subconscious willing demands of a triune soul, of hunger for food, sex, and aggression without undue discomfort, dysfunction, and pain.

Saints of all sorts and times have experienced a thrill in reducing or being relatively free of the triune soul, as obsessions of hunger for food, sex and reproduction, and emotions and behaviors of aggression. Various misnomer words are used to indicate the transcendental experience, including, ecstasy, god, samadhi, and nirvana.

Benefit

While finding care in an imagined first father beginning is a bona fide psychological delusion, it does have its benefits such as making life at least subjectively safer and more worthwhile. Most existentially vulnerable individuals lack sufficient knowledge and courage to navigate the hazards of living. Subjectively accepting the existence of an intelligent first father god, encourages humans to seek answers to the problems of living.

Directing attention to a first father is to aspire toward what is higher, to learn and to know more about a real environment and life.

Monotheism is a psychological and artistic way of seeking care in the higher cerebral cortex function of the brain by using it to imagine a first father protection. The biblical Genesis story of a first father god beginning, is an artistic way of locating goodness and caring. The only real goodness, is what is conceived of and located in the cerebral cortex of the brain that artistically imagines and crafts the word portrait story of a first father god. A first father god is a way of making life and death less threatening, friendlier, and at least acceptable. A first father is a way of assigning a good intention to existence. Surely, a good first father would not intend a bad or evil existence. Despite an original good intention for humans by the first father of the biblical Genesis story, human willful intention was sufficient to override the original intent of the god for existence to be good. (Genesis 1)

The first two humans seem to have felt their original level of knowledge bestowed on them by the first father, was woefully insufficient. The remedy was to willfully and quickly increase their knowledge by consuming the fruit from a tree of good and evil made and planted by the first father god. The first humans then ingested good and evil knowledge into themselves by consuming the rare fruit that led to an increase of human awareness of nudity and knowledge of sexual reproduction, struggle for food, and aggression. The fruit of the tree of knowledge of good and evil also contained knowledge of how to kill humans, as Cain killed his brother Abel. (Genesis 4:8) The first father god kills many humans throughout biblical writings. By consuming the fruit of good and evil knowledge this willing ability and knowledge of the god was transferred to humans,

The good and evil knowledge stored in the tree fruit, is a metaphorical way of saying that the subconscious knowledge stored in the genealogical family tree of humankind, is what causes disobedience and conflict among humans. This is the genetic knowledge of the animating subconscious soul as an innate willing hunger for food and water, sex and reproduction, and aggression.

Amusingly simple, the Genesis story has the benefit of metaphorical artistic knowledge that the mass numbers of average persons can utilize to better comprehend and manage existence.

Separation

To locate an exclusive good in a real duality of a good and evil earthly existence is difficult to do. For monotheistic religions, the answer is simple; in the long sequence of biological fathers there must be a good first father beginning that humans are separate from through time and ethical behavior.

Since the origin of existence is imagined to be good, a person can only be near to or rejoin goodness by being good. To say that god is good, does not to refer to what exists objectively but is to say that god is a good subjective idea. The individual must be good for and to something, and in the case of monotheism, this is imagined to be a first father god. If an individual is not good and obedient to a first father then there will be punishment. Such is the monotheistic tale.

Whoever wants to reinforce their own will to survive, wants the strength that brings forth the immense visible environment and mysterious intricate life forms. Monotheistic religions imagine the origin of existence to be a first father who can assist individual survival. Realistically, humankind does not have a shared origin with one caring merciful first father god. Humans are a continuation of one uncaring and merciless and ever forceful cosmological motion of the universe, and a real and restless energy of the earth environment.

For the human brain, observation of cause and effect change and movement in the environment is often associated with human and animal willing. Monotheism likens the greater motion of the universe to the intentional willing of a first father god. The observable and powerful greater willing-like motion of a cosmological force is that which continually and ever moves the universe of galaxies, stars, and planets. Life is a continuation of infinite cosmological motion, and animated quantum particles of atoms and electrons of energy elements. Conscious and subconscious willing of the brain and body is a continuation of the willing-like motion of the environment.

Willfulness

The biblical Genesis story portrays human willfulness to be fraught with harmful consequences, so much so that for the first humans, life unexpectedly changed from all good in the first chapter, to both a good and evil and a cursed experience. Like Jewish culture, willfulness is also a component of the Greek *hubris*, meaning pride, in which the hero is overly willful, a trait that leads to his tragic downfall. Excess willfulness in both cultures is a curse of unexpected consequences.

Individual willing in life is often ineffective and can easily be entangled in situations and unforeseen complications and dangers which cannot be unwilled or resolved. Imagining the greater willing of a good first father is the monotheistic way of solving the problem of human willing that is deficient, and that also displays the excessive willing of behaviors known as evil.

The biblical Genesis story suggests that the great fault of human life is willfulness. The portrayed willing disobedience by humans is a metaphor for an animating triune soul. What is bad to an imagined first father god is what is good for the soul that exerts a real forceful will to survive by behaviors to obtain food and water, sex and reproduction, and express aggression.

The biblical story of the Garden of Eden is a metaphorical statement about humankind. The metaphor of the god represents the artistic ability of the human cerebral cortex of the brain that can imagine and create the story of a first father beginning. The imaginal god represents the real conscious human self, the cerebral cortex of the brain that imagines a first father hero who possesses superior intelligence and super strong willing.

The metaphorical story of a male god as the beginning of humankind, is a way of promoting a patriarchal tradition of obedience to biological family fathers. Willing opposition of the first father with the first humans, is set up as a stereotype that illustrates the real dynamic of familial willing opposition.

Young humans in a rite of passage of sexual maturation oppose and conflict with the authority of the older biological father. This is the existential model of experience portrayed in the biblical Garden of Eden story.

Real Original Sin

The Christian theologian Saint Augustine (354-430 CE) used the Latin term *peccatum originale*, "original sin" meaning the first use of free will and consequent disobedient behavior by humans that separated them from the first father as told in Garden of Eden story. A real human separation from what is good, differs from how Saint Augustine defines it. For Saint Augustine, the first or original sin of humans was an act of willful disobedience. The consequence of obtaining more knowledge from ingesting the tree fruit, is that all humans inherited a concupiscence of excessive physical lust and desire that contributes to the *massa damnata*, a condemned crowd. The act of disobedience resulted in a permanent stain of imperfection and good and evil in the lives of the first humans. This marred and impure condition, is passed on to all individuals thereafter, and separates them from the pure goodness of a first father god.

For monotheistic religions, separation from what is good, is conceived to be a first father god. Saying that god is good, does not to refer to what is objective but is to really say that god is a good subjective idea. There is a willing behavior of human struggle to attain or avoid in the external environment, as a response to a willing internal struggle for food and water, sex and reproduction, and aggression.

Over time, life is suddenly or slowly beat down, increasingly exhausted by a willing force inside the body to exist and survive, and externally by willful opposing fellow humans, other life forms, and the willing-like change of the environment. To better assist in the willful struggle of living, a first father is artistically portrayed in the word art of monotheistic story. Over the years, the monotheistic artistic word portrait of a first father god has been slowly and subjectively accepted to be the imagined origin of existence.

Saint Augustine's foolish acceptance of the artistic word portrait story of a first father god is no longer acceptable. In contrast to use of the term by Saint Augustine, of separation from an imagined first father god, the original sin of human separation from what is real is multifaceted. The dynamic of the first sin of separation is to imagine the origin of existence to be a first father god. Original sin began as a psychological separation within the cerebral cortex of the authors who wrote the biblical Garden of Eden story.

When the Genesis authors began to look away from the real earth and sexual reproduction back in distant time, to imagine the artistic word art story of a first father god, this is the original sin of separation from a real human origin. When the subjective story was accepted through passing years as objectively true, this further added to the wide gulf of separating sin. Monotheistic religions sin by artistically imagining the origin of existence to be a first father that exists separate from the environment and humans. Humans continue to sin by separating themselves from the reality of where life originates.

Parents pass down the original sin of separation from the environment to children and other adults via the teachings, traditions, and rituals of monotheistic religions. Instead of the environment, attention is directed to an artistic imagined word portrait of a first father god. As a result, human knowledge remains faulty and fails to apperceive a first father god to be the result of artistic imagining and story.

The real sin of separation by humans from their origin is to subjectively imagine it to be a first father god. This creative cognitive mistake, a monotheistic delusion, is comforting to many yet at the cost of the reality of an animating soul that is a continuation of the energy elements of the earth, and a cosmological force that ever exists on its own.

The activation of life is not accomplished by an ancestral first father god. Life is activated as a continuation of energy from the earth. A monotheistic first father is a visage for the real energy particles of the earth from which comes living growth and movement. The false face of a first father god reduces to a mere unimportant spectacle, a real cosmological force that moves the universe.

The real original sin of separation is a cognitive failure to comprehend where life comes from. Middle East and Western monotheistic religions have long neglected to trace humankind's true origin to the earth environment. Animated by a monotheistic first father from the dust of the earth and afflicted with death, human life is regarded as insignificant while the beginning of existence is glorified to be a god.

Monotheistic oriented humans further separate themselves from what animates life by failing to observe a real existence of an animating soul. Biblical authors recognize a first father to animate life and do not recognize an animating soul to exist. This leads followers into a dark maze of monotheism that insists on a primitive and bizarre body resurrection, in which the original parts of the body will be reanimated by the first father god.

To maintain the artistic view of a first father god and to maintain sacerdotalist power and financial influence over the lives of the untutored masses, theologians continue to insist on the ignorance of a body resurrection. Theologians claim and falsely promise that they represent the power that can to this.

The dynamic of the sin of separation is to not observe an animating soul. In the Genesis story, humans first received an animating breath and free will of life but no soul is mentioned. Monotheistic knowledge and judgement is faulty as it overlooks and fails to observe an animating soul within the human body. Perpetuated by authorities and adherents of monotheistic religions, this failure continues to this modern day.

In contrast, having little knowledge of theological tenets, adherents of popular or folk monotheism continue to loosely insist on the existence of an animating soul. Despite the monotheistic emphasis on a body resurrection, many members of monotheistic folk religion also insist they have an animating soul, popularly believed to have been made by a first father god. This Christian folk view is a combination of monotheism and a vague sensing and unarticulated experience of a real animating soul of life.

In this sense, anecdotal folk reports of a real animating soul are more true than monotheistic doctrine of a body resurrection.

It is generally recognized that humans are also separate from the goodness of their full potential. Humans have known for a long time that they are capable of being healthier, living longer, and obtaining a higher level of knowledge. Indeed, humans are separate from their full potential of the goodness of health, longevity as enviously imagined in bible story, (Genesis 5) and higher levels of knowledge and wisdom.

In the biblical Genesis story, the first humans are portrayed as disobedient and as separating themselves from the higher authority of a first father god. The tale is artistically imagined and mythical, and a human separation from what is good is much better explained psychologically and physiologically. The myth of original sin also refers to the reality of human biology.

The evolved cerebral cortex of the brain has separate conscious cognitive functions that differ from the less conscious and subconscious functions of the midbrain and body. The ethical sin of separation is a failure of humans to utilize what is higher, the cerebral cortex of the brain, and instead predominantly obey the lower animating triune soul of hunger for food, sex and reproduction, and aggression. The separating sin of biology continues as the cerebral cortex functions of the brain ever differs from the midbrain and body dynamic of the animating triune soul.

Sin of God

When good differed from evil within the essence of the first father god, the resulting duality is the original sin of separation. Original sin occurred within the first father when evil differentiated from good, became separate one from the other, to affect both the willing and knowing of the first father god. Original sin of separation occurred when the distinction of good and evil formed as a duality within the willing and knowing behavior of the first father. Separation into a duality of good and evil first arose to exist within the god.

When a duality of both good and evil occurred within a singular first father, this is the original sin of separation. The opposing duality of good and evil first afflicted the father god. The first father then made and endowed the first humans with a free will made in his own image (Genesis 1:26-27). When this occurred, human free will also became afflicted with the good and evil traits of the first father's will. The first father then willed onto the earth his good and evil into the tree of knowledge.

The god sinned by separating good and evil from his own subjective will and knowledge and placing it in the objective earth environment and a fruit, where the first humans by their own willful hand soon ingested it. When the first father willingly shifted his knowledge from within to an external earthly tree, this is a sin of separating knowledge from the god to where humans endowed with a good and evil free will easily obtained it for themselves.

The free will of the first humans was of course not strong enough to take the good and evil knowledge directly from the first father but they did have the willfulness to take the god's knowledge from the tree where he stored it. Humans could not take the knowledge they wanted from the powerful first father but they could easily use their free will to do or not to do, and to take it from a tree. Easy peezy.

Human willing is free to do or nor to do. Since the first father used his own good and evil capable will to endow humans with free will to live, then humans of necessity must will both good and evil. There is no exception as human will is innately made by the first father whose own will is imbued with the qualitative traits of good and evil. The struggle of good and evil occurring within each human, is a result of an inherited free will from the monotheistic first father god.

First Sin

Differences of both willing and knowing separate humans from each other. Unfortunately for monotheistic religions, both abilities originate from a first father god.

The first biblical sin (Hebrew hata, separation) or separation from goodness, exists within the first father god as his very own dualistic knowledge and willing of both good and evil. The first father is in a perpetual state of sin as he is not all good. Evil is not separate from him, as it exists as knowledge within him that eventually progresses to willful behaviors.

In the first chapter of Genesis, the god is portrayed as only good; he makes only a good environment and living forms, and all is good including humans. The first father's own will is capable of both good and evil, and the god endowed the first humans with a free will like his own, to do or not to do, good or evil. Just like the first father, humans also have an innate ability to will both good and evil. Made with a free will in the god's image, (Genesis 1:26-27) humans from the beginning of their existence, could freely will both the good of obedience and evil of disobedience.

The primal condition of the first father's will is that it can will either good or evil, and contains knowledge of both good and evil. A sin of separation is committed by the first father when he made the first humans in his own image. By so doing the first father endowed humans with a free will like his own but not as strong or as powerful. The first father can will either good or evil, and he made humans with a free will that can disobey and oppose his own will.

The endowing of humans with a free will, immediately enabled the first humans to freely obey or not obey their progenitor. The act by the god of setting up the condition of opposing wills is a sin, a primal separation caused by the first father when he put a free and evil capable will like his own, though less strong, inside of humans. This is the original sin, and the fault is with the first father, not with the first humans.

Monotheistic authority figures suggest that humans received an all good will from the first father, and they then ruined their paradisiacal life by obtaining good and evil knowledge. Based on the Genesis story, the first humans acquired the ability to freely will either good or evil prior to an increase of pilfered knowledge.

In the second chapter of Genesis, the god's true good and evil willing character is evident with his impulsive willing into existence the Tree of Knowledge of Good and Evil. The god made and infused the special Garden of Eden tree with some of his very own evil knowledge. The first father committed a sin of separation when he placed some of his own knowledge of how to be evil in a tree fruit where humans easily acquired and ingested it. The motivation for the first humans doing so may also be traced to the first father who endowed them with a free will capable of good and evil similar to his own, and a minimal level of knowledge.

Free Will

Monotheism touts that a first father made humans with a free will. If the first humans were endowed with the capacity for a free will of obedience and disobedience from the beginning of their existence, then their disposition of strengths or weaknesses to do or not to do were given to them. How could humans have willed otherwise than they did and continue to do?

Humans cannot be totally obedient as they have an innate free will to do and to know. To be free and to be totally obedient are mutually exclusive. The capacity for a free will ability of both obedience and disobedience comes from the animating first father who originally endowed the first humans with a basic knowledge with which to inhabit the Garden. The first humans were endowed with a free will capacity to freely insist on consuming the forbidden fruit.

The Genesis myth attempts to explain the willfulness of human behavior. The real fault of willfulness is inside of individuals as an animating triune soul, a forcible dynamic of hunger for food and water, sex and reproduction, and aggression. The real development of willfulness is in the innate willing effort to survive. Humans are forced to willfully act by a hunger for food and water, by frustration to have sex, and forced by limitations to express verbal and physical aggression.

An imagined first father's willing behavior is glorified to be the all-powerful cause of the environment and life.

Unlike the imagined first father god whose willing is said to be unlimited as evidenced by the story of making the environment and life, human willing is limited. The willing of a first father is glorified as good while human willing is associated with accursed knowledge obtained from the god-made Tree of Knowledge of Good and Evil. The knowledge willfully obtained from the tree is a storied way of referring to the animating soul as a forcible hunger for food, sex and reproduction, and aggression. Though appearing disjointed in story sequence, these traits are associated with the first humans in the Garden of Eden story.

The Genesis myth is beneficial to humans in some ways, such as it explains an unknown origin. The story also benefits the average person who accepts the artistic theory of a monotheistic first father god, and who can then communicate through prayer and thereby have access to an intelligence not available in real experience. The first father god is an imagined helpmate, a way to know the unknown beginning and a way to bolster human willing to survive the environment, other humans, ageing, and death.

Artistic Tale

The biblical Genesis story of the Garden of Eden, is an artistic tale about what is higher and what is lower. What is higher is portrayed as a first father god and what is lower are the earth, serpent, and first humans.

During the early second century BCE, Jewish scribes began to translate the Tanak or Old Testament using the language of Koine Greek. The term for the Jewish word *hata*, meaning separation that occurred between the first father god and the first humans, in Greek is the word, *hamartia*, a term used in archery meaning, "To miss the mark." An appropriate term as the words of the artistic imagined story of Genesis are like arrows directing attention. The words miss the target by directing attention back in time away from immediate real experience, and outward away from the truth of where a first father is located, in the language area of the cerebral cortex of the brain.

The words of the Genesis story are arrows that miss the mark, the bullseye of truth by directing attention to an imagined external first father god rather than to an internal function of an animating soul that is a continuation of the real earth, and a cosmological force, field, or ground of the universe.

What is really being said in the artistic word portrait of a first father, is that the rational and artistic capable cerebral cortex of the brain is higher than the less rational and irrational lower midbrain and body. The conscious cerebral cortex deems it is superior as it can focus attention and make images that either measure objects in space and time and shape them into tools or weapons, or artistically portray them. Images can be objectively real or can be subjective artistic images, such as the Greek flying horse Pegasus, unicorns, Santa Claus, and sculptures, paintings, and word portraits of gods and goddesses.

Artistic story images are an inferior substitute for rational discussion. Monotheism and its artistic imaginal word portrait of a first father god is a failure to attentively observe, learn about, and intelligently discuss the cognitive processes of the cerebral cortex of the brain and the midbrain and body functions. Monotheism is also a failure to observe and to comprehend that life is a continuation of the real environment. Subjectively imagining a first father beginning who cares, is for some humans much better than what is real and now existing, the earth and the mess that is life.

The conflict portrayed in the biblical Garden of Eden, is not between a first father god and the first humans. The real struggle is between the higher conscious cerebral cortex of the brain with a lower less conscious and subconscious midbrain and body, the dynamic function of which is an animating triune soul of hunger for food and water, sex and reproduction, and aggression.

The conflict artistically portrayed in the Garden of Eden, is really between the conscious self and the subconscious soul. In Middle East mythos, the self is presented as the story character of a first father god while the soul is presented as a lowly primal serpent that urges humans.

The soul is presented as an artistic image of a serpent located outside of humans rather than inside of the body urging the first humans to know and willfully have more. The internal urges of the body are artistically portrayed both verbally and visually as the "subtle serpent," Satan, and the Devil.

Endowed with a willing ability by the first father god, the first humans became free to do or not to do, to obey or to not obey. They were given words of warning from the intelligent first father to not touch or taste the fruit of good and evil knowledge but instead listened to the less intelligent urging words of the serpent.

The tale is a metaphor, the external first father represents the internal conscious cerebral cortex. The external serpent represents the internal urgings of the much less intelligent and subconscious willing function of the body, the dynamic of an animating triune soul of hunger for food and water, sex and reproduction, and aggression. Most humans today continue to follow the urgings of the animating soul. There are those who follow the intelligent way of the cerebral cortex of the brain and learning, and those who follow the urgings in excessive and unhealthy ways for food, sex and reproduction, and aggression.

The urging of the lower serpent represents the less intelligent biological urges within the midbrain and body that persuade humans to action, and are often cursed by the higher intelligent cerebral cortex of the brain as portrayed by the god.

Recognition and respect by humans for both the first father god and the serpentine lower biological urgings must be shown, meaning both the cerebral brain functions and the appetites and functions of the midbrain and body. Both functions require individual comprehension, respect, and moderation. The conscious cerebral cortex can reason and find ways to heal the body with medicines and procedures. The subconscious soul heals wounds and can via the immune system, overcome some bacterial and viral infections.

A first father god is the artistic attempt to explain the origin of the environment, life, and the long procession of many previous biological forefathers. In monotheistic religions, an imagined first father is the force that made the first humans to exist and to live. What really forces a person to live is an animating soul as a hunger for food and water, sexual reproduction of forefathers, and aggression. Not a first father god but as a continuation of forceful energy from the earth, an animating triune soul wills and forces life to live.

Story Gist

The mythical Garden of Eden story announces two real truths. Human life is often a failure to will good, and the human search for knowledge is often disappointing and even harmful as it is not just good but is often cursed with evil consequences. Using metaphorical characters, the imagined artistic story is an immature cognitive attempt to state experiential and psychological truths of existence.

The Genesis story conveys the meaning that existence is a struggle of wills and willing behaviors. The story supposition that humans received a good free will from the first father is just not the case at all. Made by the first father who wills both good and evil, humans also will both good and evil. The word evil means, "Excessive force of behavior that causes harm, injury, suffering, and destruction." The first father reveals the evil side of his will in three instances:

Endowed humans with a good and evil capable free will like his own (Genesis 1:26-27)
Made the tree of knowledge of good and evil (Genesis 2:9)
Inflicted evil curses on the first humans (Genesis 3:15-19

The first father's will, contains both good and evil with which he first endowed humans. The god caused further injury and harm to humans when he placed evil knowledge in a special tree. Humans then willfully took the fruit from the tree made by the god, and put good and evil knowledge inside their own body. For their behavior, the god punished humans by cursing them with various evils.

With evil innate in an endowed will, obtaining godly knowledge of evil and ingesting it, and the evil inflicted by the curses of the first father, humans really had no chance to be completely good. The scenario suggests that evil is a necessity of existence.

Humans were made with a good and evil will, obtained a measure of both good and evil knowledge from the first father's tree, and were imbued with curses from the god that inflicted the evil of excessive force and grievous emotional and body harm. A curse is defined as, "an intentional application of excessive force and consequent harm." The curse of the first father god represents the countless real acts of sexual intercourse by many forefathers and foremothers that has cursed all of humankind to the good and evil struggle of life and the rigor mortis and decay of death.

The separation from the first father occurred through willing, the god's will versus human willing. Having a free will like the first father, human willing is faulty as it innately contains the ability to do good as well as evil. With the potential to freely will either good or evil, there exists a spectrum of various willing behaviors. Willing can be good but it can just as easily be a blend of both good and evil, and can also be excessively forceful and therefore evil.

A free will can be volatile, rapidly changing to or from a lax condition, balanced, or excessively forceful. It is truly difficult for humans to know how much force to exert in differing situations. When lacking a sufficient level of knowledge, then the evil of opposition and possibly excessive force is usually resorted to. To succeed in the environment, humans must exert force and it is often difficult to determine when the line is crossed from the good of balance to the excessive force of evil.

Knowledge is often insufficient to be able to adjust the level or intensity of willing effort and is frequently ignorant of outcomes. Human willing is faulty as it is dependent upon knowledge. Willing is impaired without sufficient knowledge directing it to a good outcome. Lacking sufficient knowledge, attention is directed to willfully fulfilling the urging of the soul as a forceful behavior of hunger for food and water, sex and reproduction, and aggression.

When the soul is dominant, forceful animalistic behavior predominates.

Limitation

A first father is a way of directing attention to and identifying the beginning of existence. Religious authority figures of monotheistic cultures encourage followers to accept the existence of a first father god. The ostensible intention for advocating a first father, is to have group members obey both religious leaders, and the god's alleged utterances for the purpose of having a good social order. Claiming a shared origin and having an ethical and moral supervisor of a first father god, individual members of monotheistic religion can better get along.

The ability of the cerebral cortex of the brain to acquire knowledge is limited. The human body that contains the faculty of conscious willing and subconscious metabolic willing of cellular function is limited. The poor strategy humans developed in the past to overcome limitation, and many continue to use to improve human willing and knowing, is to utilize the word portrait story of a first father god.

It is the cerebral cortex of the brain that artistically imagines and creates a first father god whose willed commandments willful humans are encouraged to follow. Subjective imagining of an all-powerful first father, is a way of empowering individuals who accept the imagined god to be objective. Imagining and associating with, and communicating with a strong first father god, also elevates and encourages the person to have personal strength.

The story of an external first father is intended as a subjective internal refuge from the external environment, other life forms, and aggressively evil fellow humans. An external god is also artistically intended by the cerebral cortex of the brain to counter the internal less conscious and subconscious midbrain and body dynamic of the animating soul of life.

For biblical authors of the Genesis story, more intelligence was needed to better comprehend their limited knowledge.

Human experience needed a higher level of knowledge about the origin of existence and it was obtained only by artistically imagining the story of a first father. The authors boosted themselves higher by imagining and writing about an intelligent first father they are related to, and who is smart and strong enough to make the environment and life.

A first father god is a way of directing conscious attention and making known the beginning of existence. The first father god of monotheism is a story character that represents the ability of the cerebral cortex of the brain to imaginatively and artistically fashion knowledge of the beginning of existence. The Genesis story is a word portrait that provides subjective artistic evidence for the beginning of the environment and life.

The biblical Genesis story tells how a first father god made a very good existence, and soon thereafter exhibited the behaviors of punishing and cursing the first humans. For humans at times, living resembles a curse to include experiences that are so unbearable that even oblivion may be sought as preferable to the miseries of life.

The true punishment and curse of life can be traced not to an imagined first father but to the very real repetitive sexual acts of many fathers that bring life into existence. This in part is what the artistically imagined first father god truly represents, the collective and reproductive forefathers of humankind.

An imaginal monotheistic first father god also represents a twofold real function of equal importance. The god represents the conscious higher-level intelligence of the cerebral cortex of the brain that can imagine the subjective origin story. The god as the animator of life, usurps and takes credit for the less conscious and subconscious functions of midbrain and body, also known as the animating triune soul, a forcible willing hunger for food and water, sex and reproduction, and aggression.

The real downfall of humankind that is metaphorically portrayed in the biblical Genesis story, is not punishment by a first father god but that life is animated by a real triune soul. While the cerebral cortex of the brain imagines a good first father god to obey, humans must really obey an internal triune soul that forces life to exist and to survive, and must obey the behaviors of the environment. The roots of the soul are a continuation of the atom and electron energies of the elemental ground of the supporting earth, and all relative motion of the universe is a continuation of a cosmological force that ever exists on its own.

Free Will Story

In the biblical Genesis story, the first father god willed the environment and living forms into existence. The god also willed the first man from the red soil of the earth and named him Adamah, meaning red earthling, alluding perhaps to the mineral red ochre which from late Paleolithic times is historically associated with life. The first father then proceeded to will the first woman Eve from the body and rib of the man.

Since the first father of the Genesis story is a god, he has an unrestricted free will. The first father freely willed the environment and life into existence, and made humans in his own image. (Genesis 1:26-27) The English word will, (from the Old Norse vija, meaning, to do, doing) is generally defined as:

"The ability of mental and physical deliberate and purposive determination, consciously or subconsciously intending and forcefully choosing a course of action or behavior."

In the Genesis story, willing is an ability to do or not do that must have been formed when the first father breathed into and animated the first human. (Genesis 2:7) The man was then animated to move and to be alive. The first father breathed into the man his nonvisible animating breath (Latin spiritus) and the man willfully moved his body to live and function. The first father endowed the first humans with a free will and ability for behavior to do or not to do.

When the first father endowed humans with their individual free will, this was the beginning for opposition and separation. The first humans soon willed against the first father and later against each other.

The god endowed humans with their own individual will to either do or not do, to obey or not obey. The ability for free will caused original sin (Hebrew hata, separation) as the will of the god then opposed his own will-endowed humans. Differences of willing equals sin, meaning separation. The first father solved his willful conflict with the first humans by using his much stronger will to forcefully punish them with curses and separating expulsion.

The first humans had only a basic feeble knowledge of good, and no knowledge of evil. They did have a god given free will with which to oppose the first father. In the punishment of humans willed by the first father, there is a conspicuous lack of demonstrative love for his errant willing and minimally knowledgeable first humans. If humans made a mistake, then no mention is made of it. No love, forgiveness, or atonement is mentioned for willfully opposing the first father. There is only sin (Hebrew *hata*, separation) and punishment. The god could only think to curse his first humans with the living of an often precarious and insignificant existence that continues to this day.

The first father ordered the first humans to not eat the fruit of the Tree of Knowledge of Good and Evil, and yet they disregarded the god's command and consumed it. (Genesis 2:16-17; 3:6) Human sin is not the acquiring of more good and evil knowledge but is the clashing separation of opposing wills. The first father caused and is to blame for the sin of separation. Endowing humans with a free will is the original sin of the first father, and the human sin is to freely oppose the god.

The first father god separated some good and evil knowledge from his own knowledge and placed it in a special tree. This is an act of sin, from the Hebrew word *hata*, meaning separation. When the god separated some of his knowledge from his own, and placed it to exist separate in a tree, he sinned as his good and evil knowledge was separate and no longer under his exclusive control.

The first father sinned, meaning he separated knowledge from himself and put it into a tree where unwatched by the god, humans easily obtained it. This story is artistically imagined word art, and metaphorically means that the good and evil knowledge and functions of the less conscious and subconscious midbrain and body, the dynamic of an animating soul, is no longer under control of and is disobedient to the conscious willing cerebral cortex of the brain and its ideational first father god.

Monotheistic sacerdotalists speak for what is higher in humans, and encourage individual faith (Latin fides, trust) in the subjective idea of a first father god. A god is the way the cerebral cortex of the brain identifies what is singularly good, in the dualistic good and evil experiences of life. The first father god is portrayed as making everything good, except for a special tree bearing a fruit containing some of his own good and evil knowledge. This act by the god is a sin, a separation from all good, to the first mention of evil knowledge. The god puts evil on the earth but humans are cursed for acquiring it. If the first father is all good, he would only have knowledge of good and would never expose humans to evil knowledge or behavior.

Real Separation

What a load of manure and nonsense is monotheistic theology. What a waste of time and effort is the delusional discussing and speculating on a first father. The real monotheistic sin of separation is the artistic imagining of human origin to be a good god. This is a psychological maneuver offered by monotheistic authorities to adherents as a pragmatic way to protect themselves from the risks, dangers, and evil situations of the earth. Those in charge of the word portrait of a good god, convince those who foolishly accept this way to good that there is a charge to those so assembled to make monetary offerings in the collection plate.

The metaphorical separation between the characters of a first father and the first humans portrayed in the artistic imagined Garden of Eden story, represents a very real separation between the human cerebral cortex, and the midbrain and body.

The god is a character that represents higher conscious reasoning and willing of the cerebral cortex. The first humans represent the afflicted willful and less conscious and subconscious midbrain and bodily need to eat, to have sex and the fruit of reproduction, and to express aggression.

A real separation occurs within the total eighty-six billion neurons of the human brain. The cerebral cortex contains only sixteen billion neurons that are intelligent and capable of conscious attention and reasoning. The other seventy billion neurons of the cerebellum and midbrain, are unintelligent and are not capable of conscious attention and reasoning. The cerebellum and midbrain neurons are less conscious and have subconscious functions as the autonomic nervous system.

The willing effort of the biblical authors of Genesis to know the origin of existence, produced picture imagery of story in the cerebral cortex of the brain, as an artistic way to explain the metaphysical origin of the physical environment and life, and good and evil experience. The character of the first father represents the cerebral cortex that artistically imagines the origin story, and the first humans represent the less conscious and subconscious midbrain and body.

Representing the cerebral cortex, the first father gets false credit for animating life, while as a continuation of the environment, the triune soul of the midbrain and body is the unrecognized true animator. Willing as the activity and movement occurring in the brain and body functions, is a continuation of the behavior of atom and electron energy particles and elements of the earth, and is a continuation of the behavior of a cosmological force that moves the entire universe and ever exists on its own.

The willing of life is a dynamic function that animates and insists on effort of behaviors, and is a continuation of relative movement from the energy particles of the environment. The word will, like the word mind, are both terms for the dynamic function of brain and body.

Willing occurs in the conscious cerebral cortex of the brain in conjunction with the dynamic of knowledge as images of remembering, imagining, deliberating, planning, and committing, leading to a conscious course of action. Midbrain and body functions are a subconscious willing of cellular and organ function of heartbeat, blood circulation, breathing, and digestion. Willing is the ability for an act of behavior, to consciously or subconsciously want to be, do, or have.

Willing

The story that a first father god with an all-powerful free will made humans with a free will, is an artistically imagined story version of existence. In the biblical Genesis tale, the first father god designed humans and made them in his own image. The first father has an extra strong will to do or not to do, and he made humans with a much lesser will to do or not to do.

The free will of a first father god must have none or few restrictions. The human ability for free will, while a limited version, came from the will of the god. Made in the image of the first father, a version of the god's free will was transferred to the first humans. In fashioning humans to have a will in his image, the first father was to make much later trouble for himself and humankind. The original sin of separation that occurred in the Garden of Eden is committed by the first father who endowed humans with a free will. The will bestowed on humans, is the mechanism that enabled them to sin, to separate themselves from the first father by being disobedient, by not willing what the god wanted them to willingly do.

A free will is an ambivalent experience. A good feeling comes from being willingly obedient to family and society, and a good feeling comes from being willfully disobedient and doing what an individual wants to do. This is the good and evil of a free will that of necessity can do either, despite what is demanded. The first father endowed humans with a strong enough will power to do the opposite of what he expected of them.

If an individual will, is free, it must be unhindered by undue limitations and the limiting admonitions of elders so that an individual can learn on their own. Human willing must have been free enough, as the first humans could do otherwise than what the god ordered them to do. The first father could have better regulated the amount of will he endowed humans with, and better adjusted it to a level where human will would not have been able to oppose and be disobedient the god. The first father made a faulty human will, as he failed to balance human will, in such a way that the first humans would willfully get along with the god and with later fellow humans.

Having a free will, there is as much willing to disagree as there is to agree. Wills do not always agree, and since they are free, willful humans can agree but can just as easily disagree, and will to differ and to go in a differing direction. This is the scenario in the Garden of Eden story. Willing is the great bringer together and just as prevalently, the great separator. Therefore, the free will bestowed on the first humans is not an entirely good product.

Individual human willing is free to agree or disagree and to differ, and this is the sin of separation. There are differences of willing between male and female, parents and children, sibling and sibling, and young and old. Evil is to will forcefully and excessively in an opposing direction. The first humans willed excessively but not forcefully in their own favor and differed from the willing of the first father.

In the Garden of Eden story humans are portrayed as far too willful, and yet if the god adjusts human willing to a less forceful level, can the will be considered as free, or should it be considered as regulated, manipulated, and unfree? A free will only enables humans to freely change behavior within limits, to do or not to do, to be obedient or disobedient, to be good or evil. While knowledge may be faulty or evil, it is the will that is the deed doer.

It is an unregulated human free will endowed by the first father that is the separating sin, the real complication of existence. The god endowed humans with a free will of good (obedience) and evil (disobedience).

Free will is the ability to do or not to do, to be obedient or to be disobedient. To always be obedient is to not have a free will. Human will must function as intended by the first father god, must be free to be both obedient and disobedient. Having a god-endowed free will, must include the ability for disobedience or human will is limited and is not free.

Good human behaviors are those that obey the first father, while evil behaviors oppose the god. Good and evil opposing behaviors originate from the free will of the first father god and from the free will that he endowed the first humans with. Evil is the excessive force most often required to live and survive. Willing is the effort of living and knowledge is what assists life to succeed and to better survive.

The monotheistic story of a first father god artistically represents how willing got into humans. The god inserted a free will resembling his own into humans. Inserting an animating free will and minimal knowledge is an obvious sin of the first father. The imagined first father, represents a real insertion of willing life by a line of forefathers, who inserted their male penis into the female vagina during the sexual act of procreation.

The biblical writers of the Garden of Eden story in the book of Genesis, utilized and imposed guilt on their fellow Jews, by imagining willful human disobedience to a first father god. The biblical story of the opposing wills of a first father and the first humans, is an exaggeration and artistic embellishment inspired by and based only upon real conflict with paternal ancestors. The imagined willing of a first father really represents the willing of many biological human forefathers. Many wives, sons, and daughters have been disobedient to many forefathers that are represented by the imagined first father of story. What is portrayed in the Garden of Eden story is an archetypal willful patriarch and a family spat of disobedience that continues today in most families.

The first father must have lacked knowledge of future consequences when he designed and placed a free will in his first humans.

Made in the god's image, the first humans were given a sufficient free will and yet were endowed with only a basic and insufficient level of knowledge of outcomes. The first humans wanted more knowledge, even if it was a blend of good and evil obtained from the fruit of a tree. The god gave the first humans enough free will to be disobedient and to acquire some of his reserved and stored good and evil knowledge.

The first father caused the sin of separation by endowing the first humans with a free will. Sinful separation was not caused by humans obtaining more knowledge but by the god when he endowed humans with a free will. Endowed with a free will, humans used their own god bestowed will to be disobedient based on their level of minimal knowledge.

The first father god has a free will, and being made in the god's image, humans also have a free will. Not as strong as the first father's will, the only resemblance of human willing to the god's will is that it is free. Free will is the ability to will or not to will, to do or not to do, to be obedient or to be disobedient., and if the first father limited human willing to always be obedient, then humans are not free. Humans cannot will more and cannot know more than the god but can freely oppose him with willing disobedience, an ability given by the first father, prior to humans acquiring an increase of knowledge from a tree fruit. The ability for willing did not increase, only the ability for knowing more than the original basic good knowledge increased.

Minimal knowing that acquires an increase of knowledge of both good and evil is certainly a secondary fault but being endowed with a free will is the original and primary fault, the separating sin. Endowed by the first father with a free will, and made with limited good knowledge, the first humans willingly disobeyed the imposing will of the first father, for the purpose of obtaining more godly knowledge. Unfortunately, the first father stashed some of his good and evil knowledge in a tree, the fruit of which the first humans willingly put into themselves.

The original sin is the receiving of a free will, free to be or not to be, to do or not to do, to have or not to have, and to obey or to disobey.

For the god to endow humans with a will that is exclusively obedient is to be limited and not free. To always be obedient is to be unfree, and only a will that is capable of both obedience and disobedience is free. Therefore, when the first father created humans with a free will, he guaranteed a future hellish existence of opposition for himself and his progeny. Modern humans continue to deal with both, an endowed sinful and separating free will, and the increase of knowledge acquired by eating the fruit that is of necessity both good and evil. A little knowledge leads to routine experience while more knowledge often leads to an increase of willful opposition and complications of living.

Cerebral Cortex

The biblical first father caused his own troubles in the book of Genesis when he made humans in his own image and gave them a free will. This act set the stage for conflict. The sin of separation occurred when the first father god put some of his own free will into the first humans. Correctly comprehended, it is the will implanted in humans by the first father god that is the great problem and separating sin of life.

In a futile attempt to regulate the human use of willing excessive force, biblical writers imagine a first father god who punishes them for their excess wicked and willful ways. Human fault is not a separation from a good first father. The real fault of existence is having a strong willing triune soul of hunger for food and water, sex and reproduction, and aggression, and a slow evolving minimal knowledge inherited from forefathers. To counter harmful human willing toward each other, biblical writers imagine a first father god with a stronger will who can punish humans.

The fictional Genesis story metaphorically represents the true evil of existence, which is mainly a willful conflict and struggle. Conscious willing of the cerebral cortex conflicts with the less conscious and subconscious willing of the midbrain and body dynamic of an animating soul. Individual willing then conflicts with the willing of others, and with the willing-like function of environmental change.

Humans struggle with the willing of parents and children, other fellow humans, harmful living forms, and the willing-like changes of the environment from good to the excess forces of evil. If the first father's good and evil will made the environment, then the personality of the god is reflected in its functions and weather, and is both good and beneficial, and harmful and forcefully evil. Environmental conditions are changeable, capricious-like, and seemingly willful. Human willing in such a variable environment is only partially effective. Therefore, many accept the greater will of a first father god.

Since the first father's will and knowledge contain the separate and dual qualities of good and evil, original sin or separation from goodness is innate in all biological life and the environment. Existence is a paired experience of opposites or opposing conditions of pleasure and pain, hot and cold, wet and dry, love and hate, health and illness, good and evil, and life and death.

The behavioral conflict of humans with the first father represents a story of the origin of perpetual existential willing conflict of a free will to do or not to do. The sin of separation came about as a clash of wills between the first father and the first humans. A first father willed the first humans to have a will of their own, and this act set the stage for familial separation.

The biblical Genesis story is a metaphor for the separating evolving split of the cerebral cortex of the brain from the functions of midbrain and body. The willing opposition of the conscious cerebral cortex of the brain with the willing function of the less conscious and subconscious midbrain and body, is the real biblical problem of sin and separation. It is the biblical writer's lack of knowledge that fails to recognize an animating soul of the midbrain and body that forcefully and excessively opposes the moderating influence of the cerebral cortex of the brain. Humans can will to be obedient to the first father god, a character who represents the cerebral cortex of the brain. Or humans can be disobedient by ignoring the higher functions of the cerebral cortex in favor of the lower midbrain and body functions, the dynamic urging of an animating triune soul for food, sex and reproduction, and aggression.

Humans have the flaw of a lower less conscious and subconscious willing cellular function of the midbrain and body, and an evolved higher god-like willing of the cerebral cortex of the brain. Both lower knowing and higher knowing cause a separating conflict within an individual, causes conflict with others as exemplified with the familial situation of the first father god and the first two human offspring, and ever after among descendants.

The less conscious and subconscious midbrain and body dynamic of cellular willing function is an animating triune soul of hunger for food and water, sex and reproduction, and aggression. This dynamic often opposes the conscious willing of the cerebral cortex of the brain, the locus of imagining a first father god. The less conscious and subconscious willing of midbrain and body perplex the conscious cerebral cortex of the brain and its god-like ability for picture images, learning, reasoning, and inventing.

Conscious willing and knowing are a dualistic interdependent function but willing is primary. Knowing is secondary and guides willing. Human forefathers and mothers were not animated by a knowing god but then as now and always, are animated by a will to live, the dynamic of which is an animating triune soul of hunger for food and water, sex and reproduction, and aggression.

Good Will

In the book of Genesis chapter one, the willing of the god is all good. Willful conflict of any kind is conspicuously absent from the story. Conflict is portrayed as an intrusion into existence caused only by willing disobedient humans.

The first mention of evil, suddenly appears in the willing of the first father as he makes a tree of knowledge that contains both good and evil. By the time of chapter two, the first father willingly makes a tree to contain some of his own good, and his own evil knowledge that he did not endow humans with. While the god usually gets credit for willing only good, he did will and make the good and evil tree of knowledge.

In Genesis chapter one, the first father is portrayed as an innocent, with a purely good will that makes all things good. Suddenly in chapter two, it is revealed that the first father does not exclusively will good but can just as easily will evil. Without explanation and in a whim-like fashion, the first father suddenly makes a good and evil tree, and leaves it to be unguarded and of easy access to humans.

The situation begs a question, why did not the first father post the guards of the cherubim as he did to block the way back into the garden of Eden? (Genesis 3:24) Blocking the way to easy access to the garden, the first father god sinned by separating even further from humans, a sinful separation lasting to the present day and time.

Origin of Evil

Knowledge of good as well as evil exists within the monotheistic first father, and he did knowingly place some of it in a tree. Yet it was not acceptable to the biblical writers and later readers and hearers of the story to assign full blame to the god for how evil came to exist within the tree fruit, humans, and abroad on the earth.

To bring blame to humans the god removed some of his own good and evil knowledge and placed it in a special tree where it was very noticeable to humans in the garden environment. (Genesis 2:9) The god sinned by not doing his best to conceal his tree of good and evil knowledge from humans. The god placed the tree containing not only his good but also his evil knowledge prominently in the center of the Garden of Eden. The enticing tree fruit is a setup, a clever literary way to incriminate the first humans who only wanted more knowledge for themselves and their progeny. The first humans had only a minimal kindergarten or early grade school level of knowledge, and the god's subtle serpent who urged and persuaded them to consume the fruit was the smartest word-using beast the god had made. (Genesis 3:1) No fair contest of knowledge here.

The god is portrayed as all-knowing and blameless. The role and responsibility of the first father in bringing evil into existence is reduced by having his smartest beast of the field, and his humans with minimal knowledge interact.

The first father is portrayed as not deserving of any blame whatsoever. It was the smart snake and barely knowing humans that are to blame, not an all-knowing first father god.

The first father endowed humans with such a minimal level of knowledge, (Genesis 2:19-20) no distinction between good and evil existed for them. The willful humans could not wrest more knowledge from the all-powerful will of the god but to remove a knowledge-containing fruit from a tree is easy peezy.

Sin

If there exists only good in the will and knowledge of the portrayed first father god, then the first humans and all later individuals would have a good will and only good knowledge. But there is not all good in the will and knowledge of the first father god, there is also evil.

The preexisting duality of the separate qualities and traits of good and evil in both the will and the knowledge of the first father is the original sin of separation. The good of the god is the ability and knowledge to make the environment and life. The willful ability and knowledge for excessive force is the evil of the god. Separating sin occurred when the first father made the first humans in his image and included a free will like his own. The duality of a good and evil free will of the first father was transferred to the first humans. The first humans inherited their free will from the free will of the first father when he made them to exist. Endowing humans with a version of his own free will, containing the dual potential of good and evil, is a primal sin of separation.

The duality of good and evil preexisting in the primal will of the first father god, is the original separating sin. A further separation occurs in the differing of will from knowledge, and willing from knowing. Whereas the first father has a free will ability to do either good or evil, the two opposing and separate qualities and traits of both good and evil must exist in a state of tension and conflict within the personality of the first father.

The differing qualities and traits of good and evil existing in the same location within the first father, as opposites must exist in a state of tension if not conflict, as it surely does in humans made in the god's image.

Located in the willing and the intelligence of the first father, good and evil must be distinct from each other as potential and willing behaviors. There then exists, the inherent necessity for a first father and humans to will either good or evil; but will they must. Since good and evil exist in the primal willing of the first father, and since the god willed all things to exist, then good and evil of necessity permeates all of existence.

The faculty of will is free in its ability to change. A will is free only as an ability to change direction from good to evil or vice versa. The inherent problem with willing or a will is, it is changeable and quickly changes along a range of options of choice ranging from good to the excessive force of evil. Since the first father gave humans their own willing existence, willful conflict has not ceased for humankind or for any other species of life.

In Genesis chapter one, the first father is portrayed as saying that everything he willed and made was complete and "very good." (Genesis 1:31) The first father could not have endowed humans with a good free will, as his own will is both good and evil as evidenced by his actions. The judgement that all is good in the making of the environment and life, is that of an author artistically portraying the imagined character of a first father. The evil side of the first father appears in chapter two of Genesis when the first humans are formed and the tree of good and evil knowledge is made by the god.

Willful effort of the first father made good to coexist with evil in a special tree. The tree of knowledge of good and evil is the outcome of willing and knowledge of the god to make it. Since the first father knows how to make a good and evil tree of knowledge and does so, then good and evil reside in both the first father's knowledge and his will. The god having willingly made a good and evil tree, good and evil must also reside innately in the willing of humans prior to their secondary obtaining evil knowledge from the tree.

The first father did not endow humans with a one-hundred percent pure and good free will. He made humans with a facsimile of his own which contains the ability for willing and knowing both good and evil.

The primal will of the first father contains a mixture of both good and evil, and when the god inserted a free will into the first humans, they too were contaminated with willing both the good of obedience and the evil of disobedience. With a facsimile lesser equivalent of the first father's will, humans were innately imbued with a capacity to do both good and evil. Acquiring good and evil knowledge from a tree only compounds, botches, and exacerbates the problem of willing.

If the god can will good and evil, and humans are made in the image of the first father, humans were made with the preexisting and innate ability to will both good and evil. The god installed a version of his own will in humans prior to them obtaining good and evil knowledge. Having a free will like the first father, human willing is faulty and tainted with a propensity and ability to will both good and evil.

In the Garden of Eden story, the struggle of wills between the first father and humans began prior to the acquiring of good and evil knowledge from the tree. The ensuing struggle between the first father and his humans began when he endowed them with a free will. Humans possessed a good and evil will, is evidenced by the use of their free will to oppose and disobey the first father prior to obtaining good and evil knowledge. The first humans received a faulty good and evil will from the first father. Endowed by the god with the willing ability to oppose, only then did humans obtain some of the god's good and evil knowledge. Lacking and wanting more knowledge, the first humans changed from willing the good of obedience to the evil of disobedience, as they acted on the potential of their endowed free will to do so.

The monotheistic origin of human ability for willful disobedience and obedience is traced to the willing of the first father god. The god willed humans to have a free will strong enough and it seems in retrospect even too strong, with which to obey or disobey him.

It is no surprise that being made with a free will that humans would soon exercise it. Humans have been willful for and against the god and fellow humans ever since. The first father should have thought better about the idea of bestowing humans with a free will like his own, ready capable to exercise the evil of disobedient opposition.

Faulty Will

What kind of will did the first father god create for the first humans? A will is almost continuously beset by mild, moderate, or intense existential tension and effort to do or not to do. Both are difficult, to exert effort to do, or to exert effort to inhibit willing and not to do. Human willing consists of and is often beset by ambivalence of doing or not doing.

Willing is both a conscious and a subconscious function, a tension of having to do or not to do in the inexorable moments of living. Willing to do or not to do can be said to always be a dynamic of existential tension and angst. Life is an ambivalent willing function, an innate two-sided internal or external conflict to do or not to do that leads to human separation and lack of accord.

Human willing is the existential core problem of existence. Yet the problem is not as portrayed in story, about opposing a first father god. The problem of life is with a triune soul. The essence of an animating soul is the willing to obtain food and water, sex and reproduction, and aggression. Willing is a function of force and effort. A free will is the function to oppose the environment, life forms, and fellow humans, as a strategy of effort to exist and to survive. Life opposes death, and so must willfully struggle to exist and to survive by willfully obtaining food and water, sex and reproduction, and to act with aggression. Life is forced and caused to act in this way by an animating triune soul.

Willing behaviors of life abound everywhere, and function as a continuation of the motion and change of the environment that extends to the varied living forms of microorganisms, plants, trees, animals, and humans. The will-like forces of the environment exhibit no care, only cycles of moderate, deficit, and excess of functions.

Therefore, a first father is artistically imagined and elaborated on with word art and portrayed to care and to will on behalf of human interests.

The willing-like changing forces of water, wind, weather, motion of the sun, moon, shifting earthquakes and volcanos, easily overwhelm human willing. Vulnerable to these willing-like forces, some humans respond by imagining a first father god with an omnipotent will who can, if he wants to, use his strong will to counter and control the will-like functions of the environment.

The story of a strong willed first father is intended to bolster confidence in human willing as it is at best only partially effective among the will-like changing functions of the environment. Some humans find it convenient to supplement their often feeble willing efforts with the ideational image of the stronger willing of a first father god. To ideationally reach for and to ally oneself with the imagined willing of a first father, is to transcend the forceful willing of the environment, other life forms, and fellow humans.

Garden Dynamic

The biblical Garden of Eden story, is a way the cerebral cortex of the human brain represents its own intelligence and solves its unknown origin by imagining a first father god. The cerebral cortex also represents the midbrain and body by imagining the first humans, who represent the dynamic function of the willful triune soul of hunger for food and water, sex and reproduction, and aggression.

The cerebral cortex portrays its own existence as a first father god who curses what predominantly demands and stimulates it to produce an excess of knowledge as picture images of memory and as images of potential future experience, that flow as a continuing stream through its focus of conscious attention. The cerebral cortex is often at a loss to direct and control the internal flow of picture images of knowledge through it, and to control the animating soul that prompts the many and often excess images. For many, the helpless cerebral cortex can only obtain assistance in comprehension by imagining a first father god to help. Yet the imagined first father ever fails to act, and only humans manage to speak on the god's behalf.

Obtaining no helping response, the cerebral cortex can only curse its fate of minimal knowledge, and what animated its life into existence. Yet no god has brought humans into existence but rather an internally sensed but not explained good and evil soul of life is the culprit. The animating soul is silent, communicating only to conscious attention with its forceful urges to live as hunger for food and water, sex and reproduction, and aggression.

Tree Fruit

Said to be omniscient, a first father must know what evil is and how to will it into existence. The willing of an all-knowing god knows what good or evil are, and willed some of his good and evil knowledge into a special tree. Besides a stern warning, (Genesis 2:17) the first father of Genesis took no special precautions of preventing the first humans from acquiring the fruit from the special tree. The god failed to post a few cherubims to guard the tree and its fruit as he did remember to post and arm them with flaming swords to guard the way back into the Garden after banishing the first humans. (Genesis 3:24)

The first father is portrayed as having an extra strong will to make the environment and life, and as having knowledge of both good and evil. The god did not obtain his ability to both will and know evil from some other place. Evil along with good is inherent in the first father as both a willing and a knowing ability. Evil can be defined as "the use of excessive force." The first father cursed the first humans as punishment for eating the fruit, meaning he inflicted the evil of intentional harm and excessive force.

Unfortunately, the first father endowed humans with both, a free will capable of opposing his own will, and a bare minimum of knowledge. The first human Adam, could only name animals, a kindergarten level ability, and there was no invention and not even clothes (Genesis 2:19-20;25) The opportunity for humans to acquire more knowledge occurred when the first father placed some of his knowledge in a special tree. This led humans with a free will to willfully disobey the god and to eat the fruit containing more knowledge of good, and unfortunately, knowledge of evil.

The first father stored some of his knowledge in a special tree he made to contain not just good but also evil knowledge. (Genesis 2:9) The first father made the good and evil tree and fruit of knowledge and carelessly placed it where humans could exercise their free will to disobey the god and acquire it. The tree borne fruit contained good and evil knowledge, and once ingested, influenced and increased human ability to will even more good and evil behaviors that continue to this day.

The god willed the Tree of Knowledge of Good and Evil into existence. The tree is portrayed as containing some of the god's knowledge, and the first two humans willfully took it for themselves. The god did not give the first humans his evil knowledge, with their god endowed free will, they willfully took it for themselves. Following the putting of good and evil knowledge in a special tree, the first humans are portrayed as willful thieves. Not an inspiring start for the human line.

The all-knowing first father used his all-powerful will to make the fruit-ladened tree of good and evil. Humans also used their own much less powerful free will, made by the god to be capable of obedience or disobedience, good or evil, to acquire an increase of knowledge of good and evil from the tree fruit.

The Israelite Jesus of Nazareth said, "Ye shall know them by their fruits." (Matthew 7:15-20; Luke 6:43-45)

As to what or whom the fruits of the tree of knowledge of good and evil (Genesis 2:9, 17) were meant for, or for what purpose is unknown. The tree must have had more than one fruit, and some of the fruits, like all other fruits do, decayed and fell to the ground and were absorbed into the soil, or were consumed by animals. Following this likely scenario, both good and evil soon permeated the environment and through the food chain to all of life. The fruit must have contained the knowledge that awakened the evil of all life as an inner demanding hunger for food and water, sex and reproduction, and aggression. The biblical god of Genesis is known by his fruits, and what fruits they are!

The first father, capable of willing both good and evil, willed all good fruits but then suddenly, and without explanation, willed the fruit of good and evil knowledge and placed some of it in a fruit- bearing tree where it was easily acquired by minimally knowledgeable and god endowed free-willed first humans. The free will ability given to humans to will the good of obedience or the evil of disobedience, becomes finally paired with good and evil knowledge. Humans ever since exactly mirror their first father god, a situation exemplified and confirmed by the saying, "The apple does not fall very far from the tree."

Genealogy

In the Garden of Eden, humans willfully put a fruit from a god made tree into their bodies that caused an immediate increase in both good and evil knowledge and behavior. The good and evil fruit willingly made by the first father god and ingested by the first humans, represents an innate animating triune soul. Prior to ingesting the fruit, there was no hunger for food as all was provided by the god. There was no sex or reproduction, and there was no aggression. Following the eating of the fruit, humans hungered for and had to provide their own food by working for it, sex and reproduction began, and so did aggression. (Genesis 3) The god's good and evil knowledge was placed in a fruit, is to say the knowledge contained therein was the sexual reproduction of life. (Genesis 30:2; Psalms 127:3; Deuteronomy 7:13; Isaiah 13:18; Hosea 9:16; Luke 1:42) Innate in life is also hunger for food and aggression to obtain it and defend fragile existence.

In the biblical Garden of Eden story, the first father willed into existence and placed some of his own good and evil knowledge in a special tree. Humans increased their original minimal knowledge not by obtaining it directly from the first father but indirectly from where the god stored some of his good and evil knowledge, in the fruit of a tree. Instead of planting more of his own knowledge in humans, the god planted it in a special tree.

The tree is a metaphorical story image. The metaphor of the imagined tree represents a real family tree of accumulated conscious and subconscious genetic memory and biological knowledge of evolved functions of how best to survive in the repetitive willing efforts to obtain food and water, sex and reproduction, and aggression. This dynamic is otherwise known as an animating soul. The imagined external will of a first father god, is a metaphor for an internal animating soul of willing for food, sex, and aggression.

The Tree of Knowledge of Good and Evil is a family tree, a genealogy of reproductive forefathers and mothers. In the Genesis story, a first father punished and forced humans to survive. In reality, humans like all of life have evolved from the good and evil environment and willfully struggle daily to exist and to survive. What the tree contains is the good and evil knowledge, not of an imagined first father god but of an animating soul that is a continuation of the real earth. Life evolves animated by elements of energy particles, and the universal motion of a cosmological force.

The first humans received their good and evil knowledge of how to survive, not from a first father god, meaning the cerebral cortex but from the midbrain and genetic heritage of the physical body. The tree represents a family tree of inherited good and evil knowledge. The family tree contains the genetic lower knowledge of survival, the dynamic willing triune soul of hunger for food and water, sex and reproduction, and aggression. Choosing to have the fruit from the tree of knowledge of good and evil, is the fruit of the womb, (Genesis 30:2) to continue to reproduce and to pass along the lower genetic knowledge of life and death.

The fruit of good and evil knowledge is obtained from a real genealogical family tree. All evolved humans have both, good knowledge from the conscious cerebral cortex of the brain, and evil knowledge of biological urges of the midbrain and body, the dynamic function of an animating triune soul of hunger for food and water, sex and reproduction, and aggression. An imagined god cannot save or enable humans to survive but an evolving cerebral cortex of the brain does increase the odds by invention, as does an animating triune soul that is resistant to destruction.

Human Will

Theologians of the monotheistic religions of Judaism, Christianity, and Islam, are in unanimous agreement that a first father god, endowed humans with a free will. This notion is also popularly acclaimed among followers of these religions as well. In the theology of monotheistic religions, there is a significance and importance that is glossed over by not focusing more in depth on the importance of human free will, such as what it is and of what qualities it may consist.

Monotheistic theologians fail to recognize, discuss, and draw an important conclusion from the Genesis Garden of Eden story, and that is the first father god made humans in his own image (Genesis 1:26-27) and endowed them with a free will derived from and similar to his own. Theologians have long committed an egregious sin of separation by not emphasizing that human free will is derived from and is a continuation of the monotheistic first father's free will.

The monotheistic religions have gotten life all wrong. In the Garden of Eden story, the ingredients of the human body came from the soil of the earth but the animating will, came from the first father. (Genesis 2:7) Monotheistic religions have imagined and written about a first father existing external to the human body and portray the god as the animator of it. In contrast, a real willing soul exists internally to animate and to contribute to individual survival of earthly life, and may also continue to animate an individual after physical death.

The metaphorical story of Genesis, and its mention of the act by the first father god breathing into the first human is important, as it suggests a special connection between the origin of existence and the animating of life. However, the real story should be, what was it that is placed into the first human to bring him to life, and to have a free will of his own?

Monotheistic adherents fail to attribute any special significance to the first father making the first human in his own image, (Genesis 1:26-27) except to apply recognition to making of the physical body.

What is grossly ignored, is that the first father god also made human free will in the image of his own. The god would have used his own free will as a model to fashion human free will. He fashioned human will to be free like his own, only with much less capacity for strength, power, and knowledge. The wills of the first father and first humans differ in abilities but cannot be radically dissimilar and they must share the same essence. Since the first father and his will is said to be eternal and not destructible, then human free will must also resemble this quality in some way. Like its first father origin, the supernaturally endowed human free will is not natural, biological, or of the earth.

Theologians through the ages have failed to notice and comment on, since the first father's free will is not destructible, human free will must resemble this quality in some way. Obviously, earthly humans do not have the willful strength and power of a first father god. Human free will was made in the image of the first father and implanted by the god in the human earthly body.

The first father's free will is accepted to be indestructible. Since human free will was made in the image of the first father's will, is human will also completely indestructible? To what level and percentage of the first father's free will, might the image of free will be in humans? Is human free will completely indestructible like the first father's or does human free will have only a percentage? Unlike the indestructible free will of the first father god, might human free will be only fifty percent indestructible? Certainly, the wills are not completely dissimilar. Made in the first father's image and human free will having been shaped by and come direct from the god, some percentage if not all of human free will, must be resistant to destruction, though the earthly body dies.

Spoken of and accepted in Hindu and Buddhist philosophies, and overlooked in the biblical Garden of Eden story, human willing is an animating soul that is resistant to destruction. In the biblical story, the artistic word portrait of an imagined first father god's will is emphasized, rather than human willing that is only recognized to be free and is cursed and condemned for its efforts.

The separating sin of monotheistic religions is the theological neglect of not emphasizing qualities of the free will of the first humans. All later humans are also made in the image of and share a likeness of the first father's free will. Humans are made in the image of the first father (Genesis 1:26-27) and therefore human free will must bear some trace of where it originated from as an inheritance. Human free will is like the first father's will, and must therefore be imbued with some degree of resistance to destruction. Yet theologians fail to emphasize the importance of human free will to be a product made in the image of the first father's free will.

Instead, theological attention usually focuses more on the physical body made from the soil of the earth and the saving of it during a future resurrection. Formed from the earth the human body eventually dies and returns to its origin. (Genesis 3:19) The body returns to the earth but what about human free will of which no mention is made? Through the years, theologians allowed the free will to perish like the biological body. However, free will is not a material or a biological quality as it was added to the earthly ingredients of the human body from the body of the first father. This I submit for due deliberation and a verdict, and suggest this is an indirect way of saying the human free will is in reality an animating soul. The theological silence on the topic is deafening with meaning.

Human free will is a version of the first father's free will. It functions in the same way, it can exert effort to do good, and it can do evil. If a first father god's free will is non-destructible, then human free will must of necessity be at least partially or completely resistant to destruction. Being made in the image of the god's will, there is a similarity between the will of the first father and the free will of the first humans and all later generations. Human will, is made in the image of the first father's will, and must have some minimum resistance to destruction.

The Genesis story reveals how the authors and redactors could not cover over what is true. The truth will out. The making of human free will delivered with a breath from the first father god, animated the first human to willfully move his body. (Genesis 2:7)

The authors did not intend to say that human free will, like the first father's will, is resistant to destruction but they could not help themselves from veering too far from the truth, and this is what is implied.

The unrecognized allusion to human free will having a resistance to destruction, is a euphemism for an animating soul that survives the physical death of an earthly body. The animating soul is real while a first father god is an artistic imagined literary character. The first father god formed the first human from the soil of the earth. Human will to freely do or not do, obey or disobey, was not formed from the earth but was only added after the body was formed. The first father god then breathed into the earthly body so that it began to live and willfully move. (Genesis 2:7) Human willing ability comes directly from and was made in the image of the first father (Genesis 1:26-27) and it therefore has a corresponding dynamic resembling the god's will.

Since free will was added to the body by and from the god and was not made from an earthly ingredient, human will would have to be a nonbiological addition from the animating essence of the first father god. The first father has a free will, as do humans who can oppose him. Analogically, just as with a biological parent a child's will shares the same essence and resembles the dynamic of the parent will, so too the will of the father and child are similar and not unalike. Whether in adult or child, wills work the same and differ only in degree of effort and ability, and supplemental learned knowledge.

The first father utilized the unearthly essence of his animating free will to animate the first humans. The soil of the earth was seemingly inert to early humans. The first father had to add an animating force to the inanimate body formed from the soil. This occurred when the first father breathed (Latin spiritus) into and animated the body to live, function, and to willingly and willfully move.

The first father breathed (Hebrew ruah) into Adam, and his body was animated to live (Hebrew nephesh) and to willingly move. The body does die as the first father warned (Genesis 2:17) the first humans.

The human body is subject to destruction as it is made from the red soil of the earth. However, human free will comes direct from the first father god, and not from the earth. The body dies but not human will, also known as an animating soul, a triune dynamic of willing for food and water, sex and reproduction, and aggression.

The unearthly will of the first father formed the human body from the soil of the earth, and then breathed into the body and it willfully moved. This means human free will is also extra-earthly and belongs not to the material earth. Free will is the ability to exert effort of the body to function and to move, and to do or not to do. There is conscious willing and less conscious and subconscious willing function of cells and organs of the body. This is of course, the overlooked animating soul, as a forceful willing for food and water, sex and reproduction, and aggression.

The free will that monotheistic theologians wholeheartedly agree exists in humans, was inserted into the human body when the first father breathed (Hebrew ruah) into the first human and he began to breathe and was then alive (Hebrew nephesh). A body that is animated, moving, and alive is then, lo and behold, a willing body that can exert effort. The will is then free to be or not to be, to do or not to do, and to be obedient or disobedient.

Jewish rabbis proscribe rituals to dispose of the physical body following death but pay little attention to an existent human will, except to blame the first humans for willfully disobeying the first father god. Few words have ever been mentioned by Christian theologians or Islamic imams about what happens at the time of death to the animating human free will obtained directly from the god. Human will, seems to be for them only biological, the effort and movement of the body, yet in story its template and function came not from the earth but direct from the will of the first father god. How can something so important be completely ignored and neglected for so long? Truly an unforgivable and serious sin of separation by humans from their origin.

Spoken of and accepted in Hindu and Buddhist philosophies, and overlooked in the biblical Garden of Eden story, human willing is resistant to destruction. In the biblical story, the artistic word portrait of an imagined first father god's will is emphasized to be special, rather than human willing that is only recognized to be free and is cursed, condemned, and defamed for its efforts. How can human free will endowed by the first father god's nonphysical will, just become nothing and decay like the physical body? The animating free will of humans is really a synonym for the animating soul that monotheistic religions completely ignore. For the authors of the Genesis story, and later theologians, only the body is real and is totally dependent on a first father animator to resurrect it.

Free Will Exposé

For monotheistic theologians, there is little significance or importance to how human life was animated and began to willingly move as a living body. The body is made from the earth, and the breathing by the first father into the first human seems to be portrayed as just a boost of breath to begin biological respiration. For monotheistic Judaism, when the body dies and breathing and willing body movement stop, that is the end of life.

Yet for the body to live, move, and do or not do, a free will that all monotheistic theologians like to insist that humans have, must have been added to the lifeless earthly body at the time the first father breathed the breath of life into the first human. The animator of life remains totally external to the body, yet a free will was transferred to the inside of the body and it willingly moved on its own to live. Yet no express mention is made of a special transfer of an animating free will. The focus of attention is completely on the first father god while the importance of installing free will in the first human is entirely disregarded. If human free will was not added to the first human at the time of the first father breathing into the body and it began to willfully move and live, when and how was it placed into humans?

The story presence of the first father represents the real origin of life that was unknown at the time.

Life is a continuation of the energy particles of the supportive earth and a too vast to be noticed nonlocal cosmological force that ever exists on its own.

Unseen animating energy is represented by the first father expiring invisible air into the lungs of the first human, to animate the life of a willing body formed from the soil of the material earth. The biblical writers of the time, and later theologians, saw no special importance to the story detail of an animating breath (Latin spiritus) coming direct from the god. In the eyes of the biblical authors and rabbis, there is nothing special and significant about the transfer of breath. Yet when the body began to willingly move and live, a free will must have been added to the lifeless body at the same time. Breathing is an autonomic function and effort of body willing.

When the first father directly breathed into the first human, the body was animated and began to willingly move. The act is important as it represents the placing a version of the god's own non-destructible free will into the earthly body of the first human and to be later inherited by all humans. The god made a human free will in his own image and placed it in the earthly human body to function as a free will. Therefore, the human version of the first father's will must of necessity also be resistant to destruction.

The Garden of Eden cast of story characters is an artistic metaphorical way of representing real external non-destructible particle energy to be the origin of an internal animating triune soul. The Garden of Eden story portrays a connection of the function of the visible material earthly body with a nonvisible immaterial origin. The real origin of life is not a first father but energy particles of which the animating soul is a continuation as a forceful willing for food and water, sex and reproduction, and aggression. Energy is the origin of the material earth and the physical body.

For monotheistic religions, the body of the first human was formed from the earth and was eventually cursed. When breathing stops and the body dies, nothing of the body survives death. An early speculation was, the shadow of the body survived and went to Sheol, the pit under the earth.

Later there developed the theology of resurrection and the belief that the original physical body would be animated to breathe natural air again.

Made in the Image

To say humans are made in the image of a god, more accurately means the image of the first father is made in the brain of the artist writer of the words of the book of Genesis. (1:26-27) The subjective word portrait of a first father god is made by the human brain and promoted by clergy and accepted by many to be objective. The only image made is by humans of a first father maker portrayed in story.

Pragmatically, if humans do not continue to subjectively imagine a first father god, individuals will then have to face the environment, other life forms, and each other alone. Humans have a minimally intelligent conscious self of the cerebral cortex of the brain, and a less conscious and subconscious midbrain and body dynamic of an animating triune soul. The worst of existence is that without a first father, humans will have to face the real animating triune soul within them. This spells trouble for humans interacting face to face. Better to imagine the face of a first father god to exist, and claim a common parental origin as protection from family fratricide.

A first father god is a subjective artistic word portrait that exists only in the human brain. Yet the metaphor of a first father god endowing the first humans with a free will made in his image does suggest something special about human willing. The importance is that human will and willing, like the will of the first father, is resistant to destruction. Human free will, is a monotheistic euphemism for an unacknowledged and unaccepted animating soul that is a continuation of the energy particles of the earth elements, and an entangled continuation of a nonlocal cosmological force.

Special

Is there something inside of the human body that animates and enables it to survive death?

The general population of the earth answers yes to the question. History is replete with many reported sightings of ghosts, deceased relatives and friends, reports of childhood reincarnation memories, and near-death experiences. Therefore, the general consensus is that something special exists within the human body that survives physical death.

In the many artistically imagined stories about a first father god, there is ensconced in the book of Genesis a small grain of truth that suggests survival after death. The first father god is portrayed as giving the first human both an earthly body and a special free will by breathing into him. Through the years, human free will was given a bad monotheistic reputation of disobedience that is blamed for bringing much physical suffering to humankind.

Throughout history little interest has been shown in the Genesis story of how and when the first father god animated the first human with a free will. Instead, more interest has centered on survival of the body. In the thinking of the early Jews, the shadow of the body went to Sheol when the body died. Later in time, interest in the resurrection of the physical body developed and continues today. Not a murmur about the free will in humans and what happens to it following death.

Coming directly from the metaphysical god and not the earth, makes the animating free will special. Free will is usually only given credit for moving the body and for the ability to do or not to do, and is cursed and defamed for the original sin of disobedience that continues to mar the purity of all humankind. What is cursed by the first father in the Garden of Eden story is the human free will that he endowed them with. Human free will is not as strong as the imagined first father's will, yet it cannot be devoid of all similarities to the god's will, and must have some related qualities such as ability to exert effort, determination, resilience, and most likely considering where it came from, a resistance to destruction.

Though the physical body made from the earth cannot resist destruction, the first father shared his metaphysical destruction resistant free will with humans.

Since human free will was bestowed by the first father and his will is deemed to be non-destructible, then human free will must have a similar quality of being resistant to destruction. A destruction resistant free will is but a roundabout substitute and synonym for the word soul. Of course, the soul as a willing hunger for food and water, sex and reproduction, and aggression does not come from inert dirt but from what was unknown at the time, the unseen energy particles of atoms and electrons of the elements. The first father is the human face given in story to represent an animating soul that is a continuation of the indestructible energy elements of the earth.

Anchored in the local energy particles of the earth, and the background of a nonlocal cosmological force, human willing is a continuation of both a local and nonlocal reality. Based on the physics theorem of conservation of energy and momentum, the dynamic of an animating soul suggests survival after physical death. There is a mountain of anecdotal evidence on reports of near-death experience survival, reported visits of the deceased to family and friends, and ghost haunting field investigations and case studies. The evidence suggests that something metaphysical within the human body exits post mortem and tends to survive and linger dimensionally after physical death.

Curse of Life

Acquiring knowledge, whether subjective or objective, academic or experiential, is the only way of banishing the harmful affliction of ignorance. Lack of knowledge is a curse on human existence. In the artistic imaginal story of Genesis, sufficient knowledge was what Adam and Eve lacked and innocently sought in the middle of the Garden of Eden. Unfortunately, with his own free will riddled with good and evil knowledge, the first father did not furnish the first humans with a tree of only good knowledge.

The tree of good and evil knowledge faithfully reflects the true condition of the first father's will, capable of not only good but also evil. The endowed free will of the first humans contains the innate evil inherited from the will of their first father.

Willful disobedience is innate and is expressed when an opportunity is presented. The sincere effort to learn and know more, resulted only in a catastrophe of curses from an angry first father, and a consequent struggle and suffering for the first humans and their descendants.

In this scenario, the metaphor of the first father represents the conscious cerebral cortex of the brain. The metaphorical first humans and serpent represent the less conscious and subconscious functions of the midbrain and body. The god's curses are the judgements of the cerebral cortex against the primary animating soul as it dictates to the first father by forcefully willing for food and water, sex and reproduction, and aggression. The angry first father's curses reveal his poor remedy and powerlessness against the less knowledgeable but primary dynamic of an animating and willing soul of life.

The biblical Garden of Eden story of Genesis portrays the first father god cursing and condemning humans. What is really occurring is the cerebral cortex of the human brain is cursing the trouble-making midbrain and body dynamic of living which is the animating triune soul of hunger for food and water, sex and reproduction, and aggression. The curse is portrayed as coming from an external first father but is really located inside the body as the internal dynamic of a non-recognized animating soul of life.

The biblical story of Adam and Eve, represents the early human plight and struggle to comprehend the origin of the environment and life. The Genesis story of a first father god is the poor result of a monotheistic answer to the question of where existence comes from. The subjective imagined story presented as objective, is a curse of primitive false knowledge, of mistaking and trusting monotheistic word art to be objective and true. Those who promote or accept on faith, belief, or tradition, the tenets of a monotheistic religion have cursed themselves with the artistic version of a first father god as the origin of existence.

The monotheistic religions that advocate the artistic word portrait rendition of a first father to be the origin of existence, betray those followers who having little knowledge of religion, can only rely on blind faith to accept the primitive theory. The curse of the knowledge pandered by monotheistic religions, is that it is false and yet is held out to the immature and gullible to be real and true.

It must be comprehended that the gods of all religions are artistic expressions. All religions have artistic costumes, dances, music, structures, sculptures, and verbal or written word portraits of a god's behaviors and demands. The monotheistic religions prefer an artistic word portrait of a first father as the maker of the environment and life.

The knowledge of good and evil obtained by Adam and Eve was soon accompanied by curses from a first father that had the effect of imposing a lasting stain or sin of separation on all humans. That life is a curse is close to the pronouncement of Siddhartha Gautama, better known as the Buddha, (circa 623-543 BCE) who observed that life is *dukkha*, meaning, ill-fit-together, consists of parts, and therefore existence is an experience of various sufferings.

Contrast the monotheistic scenario of a first father god cursing the first humans for obtaining some of his very own knowledge, with the awakened level of knowledge obtained by Buddha. Siddhartha sought for an increase in his knowledge of existence. According to tradition, after six years of effort he achieved his goal of awakening to better comprehension and knowledge of life and death. Buddha awoke, and got beyond the real curse of life, *avidya* or ignorance, based on a dismal lack of meditative attention to observe.

It is not sanely possible to compare artistic story knowledge of monotheistic word art supported only by faith, belief, and tradition, with the observational meditative methods of nontheistic Buddhism. While redacted and edited through many years, Buddhist teachings continue to be cognitively clean. The core teachings are a mental hygienic philosophy and psychology of reliable experiential knowledge supported by meditative observation.

Word Art

A word using monotheistic god of Genesis is portrayed by a human artist-author to make the story images of a word portrait. The word art of books is often accompanied by visual arts of drawings, illustrations, and photographs. This demonstrates the relationship between the two; visual and word images are both art.

In the cerebral cortex of the brain, an artist gets an ideational image of what and how to shape a work of art. To know the beginning of existence, the monotheistic word artist shapes the character and deeds of a first father god. The word artist of the opening chapters of Genesis shapes the imaginal portrait of a first father god into a story character who is portrayed as verbally shaping the environment and life.

Words said to be uttered by a first father god are the sayings of an author putting words in the mouth of an imagined story character. The first father is a word built god who variously called and spoke things into existence to make the environment and life. (Genesis 1) The word art of Genesis presents a grand stage show of successive acts of making the environment by the main character of a first father god. The artistic use of words in chapters two and three proceed to explain how human behavior went from the all good of chapter one to an admixture of both good and evil.

Monotheism is the emphasis on utilizing the cerebral cortex of the brain to use language as an art to artistically fashion the word portrait of a first father god. Art is representation, and biblical word art of the Garden of Eden story, portrays the drama of willful separation between the first father god and the first humans. Wordy curses uttered by a first father god are directed to the first humans. Realistically, the word art of Genesis represents disapproval by the cerebral cortex toward the midbrain and body and its continuing dynamic demands of an animating soul for food and water, sex and reproduction, and aggression.

Many are attracted to seeing and hearing artistic products of painting, sculpture, music, plays, and movies, while many others are attracted to reading and derive comprehension and pleasure from it.

Reading, or much more likely told about the adventures of a first father god, is the simple metaphysics of the masses.

Lament

Middle East cultures fail to develop and utilize any method to better comprehend the human condition and instead naively project a subjective ideational image outward to be a first father god who continues to serve as a poor story explanation for the at times abysmal struggle of life.

The Garden of Eden story is a lament, a song or poetic expression of grief, regret, and sorrow. The Garden of Eden scenario is a poem of regret for the struggle and grief of life, for sexual reproduction, struggle for food, aggression of killing fellow humans, ageing, and death. The poignant sorrows of living are only superficially reduced by artistically imagining a first father god. The Garden of Eden story portrays a separation of humans from a higher intelligence of a first father god but in reality, is a lament for a lack of comprehension by the conscious cerebral cortex of the human brain. The artistic story of the Garden of Eden is a symptom of a lack of a better comprehension of the causal vicissitudes of life and more effective remedies. It is a lament of a failure to develop a method to better observe and to comprehend what animates life internally, and to find better ways of reducing the sufferings of existence.

Father Figure

Experiencing the environment and life as both good and evil, provoked Semitic cultures to ponder if there were at least one thing in existence that might be all good. The direction of past time was chosen as it is distant and not available for observation, and could be easily filled with the ideational word story images of a first father god. A first father god does not actually help humans endure the ever-changing moments of time and experiences of living. It is the subjective idea of a first father god that assists many humans to endure the inexorable changing times of life and death experience.

Amusing but sad, when monotheistic authorities encourage individuals to turn to a god, they are merely urging them to turn to the origin of sexual reproduction. The first father used his knowledge of how to make genitals and endowed humans with them. The first humans then acquired knowledge of how to use their genitals from the god's special tree in the Garden.

Taking refuge in the good of a first father god is really a turn of attention in the direction of the biological reproduction of many forefathers. The first father made things with his mouth by voicing them into existence, not with his genitals. However, the first man was made in the image of the first father, (Genesis 1:26-27) and so the god must have genitals.

The Semitic effort and search for a cause was to result in an artistic illustration of words and the literary imagined story of a first father god. The beginning of existence is made known by illustrating it with words to be a first father in a sequence of time composed of many real forefathers. Taking refuge in a monotheistic first father god is to accept the imagined artistic word portrait made by the higher cerebral cortex of the brain. Imagining a first father god, is a way the conscious cerebral cortex of the brain claims precedence and superiority over the long line of biological development and sexual reproduction by forefathers. The god figure is the way the intelligent cerebral cortex asserts its dominance of conscious reasoning over the less conscious and subconscious unreasoning of an animating triune soul of hunger for food and water, sex and reproduction, and aggression.

Story

The ideational image of a first father is artistically crafted into story, and then promoted as an easy way to comprehend the origin of existence. This simple prepared pabulum for the masses serves as a guide to what is good, through the good and evil maze of daily living. From the Middle East, the monotheistic notion spread into Italy and through much of Europe to become the land of a first father ancestor religion.

Monotheism, especially Christianity, became the norm and accepted way to explain the beginning of existence. The first father god also serves as a haven from the vicissitudes of living. Accepting the artistic imagined story of a first father god is a way of justifying the struggle of life, and is a way of finding respites of personal peace. Only a species of hairless apes can possibly accept the monotheistic artistic story of a fantastic first father god as real and true.

An idea of a monotheistic first father is not a revealed communication coming from an external reality but comes from internal creative imagining, of arbitrarily placing a first father at the beginning of existence to identify an origin, and to watch over, reassure, and protect individual life. Who was the literary word artist or artists that first came up with the very illogical idea that since there are many forefathers, a first father must surely exist? Poor and pitiful logic, to say since there are so many past fathers, there must exist a first father of the sequence.

Surely in the twenty-first century of the new millennium, humankind has evolved to the stage that the faux pas story of an imagined first father god as the origin of existence, must be recognized for what it is, an artistic expression of word art. Monotheism and its emphasis on a first father, is a primitive form of an imagined genealogy, a way to identify and explain the origin of existence. The genealogy is not based on historical documents and experience but on artistic imagining and the verbal and written word art of story. A monotheistic first father god is an artistic way of alleviating the struggle of humans with each other by imagining a shared mutual parent relationship. Many continue to accept and to bask in this subjective and protective idea of a first father god.

The cause of struggle in life is not an artistic ideational word portrait of a first father god hung in the belfry of the cerebral cortex of the brain. The cause of human struggle is not curses from a first father god. The cause of strife and suffering is a real animating triune soul, a hunger for food and water, sex and reproduction, and aggression, supported by a changing environment, and the seemingly endless motion of the cosmos.

Leonardo da Vinci observed that "Art is never finished, only abandoned." This statement can be roughly applied to the artistic word art of monotheistic religions. The scriptural word portrait of a first father god as an artistic explanation for the origin of existence has long been finished, and will eventually be abandoned by an evolving human species.

Good

A monotheistic first father god is artistically imagined and functions as a way some humans make themselves feel good. Imagining the existence of a first father is a way of reducing and relieving some of the pains of life and the horrifying experiences of ageing, dying, and death. Imagining an intelligent fatherly god is a way of rationalizing a non-rational environment and irrational life experience of many difficulties and evils.

Monotheistic sacerdotalists insist they are near to the good of the universe, identified by them to be a first father god. The good behaviors displayed by clergy members serve to represent the goodness of a first father. By appealing to a monotheistic god, sacerdotalists offer refuge to vulnerable individuals, from the environment, and mistreatment by fellow humans. A good first father is a subjective shelter from the objective environment and the predatory aggression of other humans.

Guilt

Serving as legal defense for the first humans, their biblical first father failed to will and know only good. The saying, "The apple does not fall very far from the tree," certainly applies to the biblical humans who like their first father failed to will and know only good. The first humans chose to willfully acquire both good and evil knowledge from a tree made to grow by the god. The content of the tree perfectly reflects the content of the god's will to make it. Obtaining the first father's knowledge from the tree, the first humans found the content of the fruit to contain some of the god's not so good knowledge. Consuming the fleshy fruit awakened them to know more and to will more evil.

Monotheistic religions generally insist their first father god is one-hundred percent good, even though he can also punish. The first humans are blamed for acquiring the knowledge of good and evil from the first father's special made tree. Consuming the fruit awakened humans from a sheltered Garden existence to the true knowledge of how life is on the real earth. Life is both good and evil as it perfectly reflects the good and evil will and knowledge of the first father god.

The first father is portrayed as giving life, and the first humans are represented as causing death to themselves and humankind. (Genesis 3:3,19) What a burden of guilt for humans, to be accused of causing the countless deaths of young and old alike. The first father god utilized his knowledge to make humans with genitals of penis and vagina. Humans acquired knowledge from the tree of how to utilize them in sexual intercourse and this began the fleshy fruit of biological reproduction. Realistically, the first father god merely represents the long line of sexual reproduction by countless forefathers, and mother, who have made the choice to indulge in sexual behavior. The fleshy fruit of sexual intercourse is orgasm and often pregnancy. (Genesis 30:2) The ripening of the fleshy fruit of life is the ageing that bestows the rigor mortis of death on all those who are born.

Biblical artist-writers imagined a first father god to be the animator of life, and neglected to observe the demands of an animating soul within the body. The effort to live displayed in the functions of cells and organs, is an animating triune soul of hunger for food and water, sex and reproduction, and aggression. This less conscious and subconscious function evolves functions of conscious willing and knowledge. The lower knowledge of the midbrain and body directing humans to find food and water, have sex and reproduce, and be aggressive, often contradicts higher knowledge of the cerebral cortex of the brain, represented in story by a first father god.

Humans are ever separate from a lasting goodness, stranded on a changing earth environment with a precarious biology. As a continuation of the environment, an animating soul is difficult to always direct to what is good.

It is much easier by far to imagine and to accept a good first father god to be in charge of existence. Yet faith in being saved by a first father god is a misplaced trust in artistic imagined word art. The first father represents the offered mechanism of saving humans when in reality the true savior is an animating triune soul that is resistant to destruction. A first father god is the recognized dramatic actor that receives attention, adulation and applause. What really animates life, is the usually popular spoken of but less recognized soul.

Will

Through the evidence of human history, it is easy to draw the conclusion that superstition is prevalent and a general lack of knowledge is a perennial problem. Equally if not a worse problem, is that of the human will, the ability to exert effort known as willing. The most important books written through human history are those that discuss the problem of human willing. The majority of books written are poor entertainment or fictional trash.

Early humans found individual willing to often be ineffective against events in the environment, illness, ageing, and death. Therefore, they found they could at least make themselves feel better by imagining the beginning of existence to be familiar and human-like and to be a god. By so doing they could then appeal to the god who it was hoped could more effectively will for them.

The answer to the problem of human willing was to artistically imagine and sketch a word portrait of the greater willing of a first father. The problem of ineffectual or conflict-ridden human willing was superficially solved by imagining the beginning of existence to be a first father god who with his powerful will dictated commands to be followed by his descendants. The problem of human willing was poorly resolved in the Middle East by artistically portraying a first father god in a word portrait of story. A poor artistic solution to the real problems of living.

The book of Genesis is an early story that discusses the problem of human willing.

The first father god exhaled his metaphysical spirit or breath that must have included a free will, into the inert earthly body of the first human. The first father has the ability to will good or evil for human benefit. Made in the image of the god, humans also have a willing ability for either good or evil. This is the existential problem for humans during the brief sojourn of life and death. The proffered solution to the problem of willing is to follow the willful commandments of the first father god.

Early Middle East humans used their will and primitive artistic talent to imagine a human-like first father and to fabricate stories about the god. The artistic word portrait of the strong will of a first father god is utilized by monotheistic authorities to increase the strength of their own willing for importance, influence, and wealth.

Later in time, the philosopher Arthur Schopenhauer (1788-1860) wrote about the problem of human willing. For Schopenhauer, the will underlies phenomenal existence as a noumenal presence behind the ever-moving universe, and is innate in all living forms as willful egocentric desiring, longing, craving, and striving through life. A way to relieve the willful struggle of life, at least temporarily, is aesthetic sensitivity to beauty in the arts. Aesthetic contemplation of the beautiful gives a respite from the struggles of willing to be, do, and have, that Schopenhauer calls the "penal servitude of willing." Frustration of willing causes pain while contemplation of beauty brings relief and upliftment. Influenced by Hindu and Buddhist teachings, Schopenhauer advised the practice of meditation and ascetic disciplines, as ways to reduce the extremes of willing that lead to a palingenesis, the return of the will to live in another body.

The writings of existentialist philosopher Fredrich Nietzsche (1844-1900) offer a critique of historical human willing. Cultures are a clash of individual wills and group wills against each other. All living things exert their will to exist and to live, and a first father god is an imagined and human written story to explain the origin of existence and to support human willing to overcome the obstacles and struggles of life. Truth is relative and not absolute, and a first father god is only relative to those cultures that accept it.

For Nietzsche, the history of human willing is an antagonism between classes, the master aristocracy of strong willed individuals who command, and the slave class who are weak willed and obedient. The aristocratic masters of a culture use their ability to willingly command through force and making of laws, while slaves use their willing to obey and follow religious and governmental laws. An individual who exerts effort to develop willing to its fullest expression does so to develop his personal will to power, in German, "der Wille zur Macht."

With his well-known statement, *Got ist tot,* meaning, God is Dead, Nietzsche predicted the future demise of the monotheistic conceived first father. Humankind will evolve out of the immature need for a first father god figure. The new model hero who will save and guide humans will be the *Ubermench*, meaning in English the superman or overman. In the place of a first father god, Nietzsche substitutes real human potential to learn, especially in science and psychology, and to better comprehend life and the environment. Humans will learn to overcome many of their limitations to eventually develop a higher level of comprehension and ability. In so doing humankind will evolve out of the immature cognitive stage of needing a first father god to explain the origin of existence and for care and protection.

Eternal Recurrence is Nietzsche's view that there is something about the human will that may recur or return again and again. Nietzsche had a vague intimation that the will was not destructible but he did not venture to assert how this may work. He did suggest that each must love the necessity, *amor fati*, of what one wills.

A man by the name of Siddhartha Gautama, (623-543 BCE) known to history as Buddha, alone had a method to solve the problem of human willing. Through meditation and moderate ascetic practices of training attention, the Indian son Buddha solved the miasmic internal mystery of an animating willing soul through the discipline of meditation and three practices of forest living. These are the eating of one meal daily and preferably before noon, celibacy, and cultivation of compassion to reduce aggression. With these practices Buddha reduced and balanced the triune willing soul.

Buddha utilized moderate ascetic effort to reduce the animating willing soul that is expressed in each individual as a forceful hunger for food, sex and reproduction, and aggression.

Story legend recounts that that prior to his enlightenment, Buddha was tempted by Mara, a figure who according to tradition represents death. Mara does not represent the praised blissful *atma*, or soul of Hinduism; the character represents a real triune forceful soul that leads to death. Mara tempted the Buddha to distract him and to give up his quest with his three beautiful daughters, who sought to seduce him with sex.

Mara also remarked how thin Siddhartha was from fasting, and tempted him to give up his quest for enlightenment and consume food. Buddha defeated Mara or death by refusing the temptation of sex with his attractive daughters, gradually began to eat food in moderation to regain his strength, and did not react with aggression toward Mara. This metaphorical story tells how Siddhartha Gautama reached awakening to become Buddha, by overcoming the triune soul of a hunger for food, sex and reproduction, and aggression.

Blessed with the insights obtained long ago during through the efforts of Buddha, and the painstaking discoveries of modern science, it is no longer possible to claim a descent from a monotheistic first father god. Today it is possible to claim a realistic descent from an inferred metaphysical cosmological force that moves the universe, and descent from verified metaphysical energy particles of the environment. A metaphysical animating triune soul of a forceful willing hunger for food and water, sex and reproduction, and aggression, is a continuation of energy particles that confer a resistant to destruction.

Resurrection

The Nicene and Apostles Creeds of the Christian Catholic and Protestant churches both conclude with the statement of faith of looking forward in time to the resurrection of the body of those dead and of a future physical life existence. A range of polls on Christian beliefs show from sixty to ninety percent of those polled accept the physical resurrection of Jesus.

The majority do not see Jesus as having an animating soul and rising from the dead on his own but that it was an act of resurrection performed by a first father god. The convoluted doctrines of the Christian religion reveal an inept and confusing theology of the body and what survives death. Many early Christians were Jews and favored the resurrection of the body. Resurrection is in stark contrast to the the Greek and Roman view of a psyche or anima that survives death of the body and journeys to an afterlife under the earth in Hades. The gospels emphasize the physical resurrection of Jesus, and that his body survived death, not his ghost, spirit, or pneuma. (Luke 24:37-40; John 20:27)

Modern Christian denominations such as Jehovah's Witnesses, Seventh Day Adventists, Church of God, Amish and Mennonites have the view there is no soul and that the physical remains of the person rest or sleep until resurrection of the body. This includes both resurrection of the just and unjust on a last or final day of judgement. To say the body "sleeps" is amusing and perplexing as what is it that sleeps? The first father endowed humans with breathing (ruah) and a living (nephesh) body but not an animating soul.

Through the years following circa 200 CE, budding Christian theologians began to be more influenced by Greek thinking of a psyche or soul. They came to accept that a spirit, the animating breath of the person transits directly after death to an afterlife dimension. The contemporary Protestant Baptist theology is that humans have a rational intelligence, and a surviving breath or spirit and not a soul, that is judged immediately after death, with the good person entering heaven and the evil person entering hell to be punished. There they remain waiting for the body resurrection and the last or final judgement. The Baptists find sparse theological support for this view in a single gospel verse of the Greek physician Luke. Being Greek, Luke wrote for a Greek audience who were of course familiar with the view of a psyche or soul leaving the body at the time of death.

"And Jesus said unto him, Verily I say unto thee, Today shalt thou be with me in paradise." (Luke 23:43)

This statement is portrayed as having been made on Friday late afternoon or evening prior to the beginning of the sabbath at sunset. The body of Jesus was placed in a tomb just prior to sunset and the beginning of the sabbath, as was the custom. As per their lunar calendar, the Jews to this day, calculate a day as beginning from one sunset and ending at the following sunset. Therefore, one and one-half days later, early on Sunday morning, the body of Jesus was found to be missing and he appeared physically alive first to Mary Magdalene and later to others.

Protestants accept both, his reasoning surviving spirit or breath and the later body resurrection of Jesus as well. Some Baptist groups refer to what survives bodily death to be a "soul competency," obviously meaning that what survives death is completely conscious and can make rational choices. This seems to be more monotheistic babble, gobbledygook, and gibberish for a free will so often touted by monotheistic religion. The first father did not bestow a soul on humans but only endowed them with a breath, (ruah) and a nephesh, (life) that also included a free will. A soul competency means that humans have a free will and are competent and responsible for their behaviors of good or evil.

The Baptist doctrine that humans have a surviving spirit, an animating breath and free will of a conscious personality that goes directly to an afterlife of a heaven or hell, is also accepted by Methodist and Presbyterian churches. Following Baptist theology, deceased individuals wait in an afterlife dimension for the final judgement and resurrection and the rejoining of the breath or spirit with the physical body. Catholics also accept this view and add another dimension between heaven and hell known as purgatory. This is an intermediate state where sins are purged so the person can eventually proceed to heaven. The view of purgatory is nonbiblical.

Christian denominations do not approve of cremation, and insist on burial of the body so it can be resurrected at a future time. An exception is the United Methodist Church that allows for cremation and organ donation of the body. Methodists accept the resurrection of the physical body of Jesus after his death.

They also accept that following the sound of the last trumpet and resurrection of the physical body, it will be transformed by the first father to be a pneuma or an ethereal and imperishable spirit body as mentioned by the evangelist Saul or Paul. (I Corinthians 15:42-44; 52-53)

In Protestant theologies, a surviving breath or spirit is said to exist and yet is controlled completely by the first father god who as the only animator reattaches the spirit of breathing to the body during a resurrection of life. Protestant religions seem to conflate the animating breath or spirit the first father exhaled in the first human, with a free will. The monotheistic blind faith in a bodily and a breath or spirit resurrection is a dogged determination to hold onto the body in whatever condition that can be imagined.

Intuitively recognizing the importance of what Jesus said about the kingdom or place of a god to be within a person, Christian popular folk religion eventually came to accept that a metaphysical breath or spirit survived physical death of the body. However, it was completely controlled by a first father god who would someday remove it from an afterlife dimension, resurrect the body, and reattach and reanimate the physical form with the breath or spirit.

American Spiritualism

When the phenomenon of communication with a deceased person occurred near Rochester New York, in the year 1848, as many as two to three million eventually flocked to the nascent religion that came to be known as Spiritualism. The supposed interaction of the Fox sisters with a deceased peddler, demonstrated and convinced many of the reality of survival after death. This is a radical departure from the monotheistic religions of a breath or spirit and the primitive insistence on a body resurrection.

For Spiritualism, the animation of life is within and is not entirely dependent on the external authority of a first father god who will resurrect the body. Spiritualists do not use the term soul to refer to what animates life and survives death.

They prefer to use the term spirit. For the religion of Spiritualism, the animating breath or continuing spirit of life is free to communicate and wander using its own conscious free will. The autonomous animating force referred to as a spirit inside the body takes authority away from an external first father animator who completely controls any remaining after-death residue of humans.

While there is no named god in the religion of Spiritualism, an Infinite Intelligence is accepted to exist. This like a first father god, is a way of rationalizing an irrational existence of semi-orderliness, and an irrational animating soul as a hunger for food and water, sex and reproduction, and aggression.

True Religion

Hominin species began to evolve on the earth some seven to nine million years ago, and eventually evolved into modern Homo sapiens. During this long stretch of time, an aesthetic sensitivity and creative impulse developed to make tools and weapons. The making of visual art developed along with its twin religion. Indeed, religion is an artistic expression of images, whether of sculpture, painting, or word art that tells a story.

There is convincing evidence for this assertion extending far back in time. When Paleolithic humans entered European caves circa 40,000-10,000 BCE, predominantly in France and Spain, they often did so with the pragmatic intent to draw images of animals and sometimes plants. Entering the caves, early peoples were making a religious pilgrimage to the origin of life.

In retracing life to its origin in the interior of the earth, Paleolithic humans were imitating the observed origin of life from within the body of the mother. The vaginal opening and womb within the human female body was likened to the opening of caves leading into the mysterious interior of the earth accepted to be the origin of life. Early humans drew an analogical parallel of the human body with the earth.

Early humans had to have been curious about what was within the female body from which life came from.

Aside from observing pregnancy and birth, a pregnant woman unfortunately may have been disemboweled in an accident or act of violence by animal or human, and the fetus would have been observed to exist inside the mother. Yet a mystery remained of how the young got into the body of the mother.

Early humans acted out a return to the origin of life by entering particular caves. There they drew images of parietal art, on the floors, walls, and ceilings of the cave. This behavior can best be explained by the Petitionary-Midwife Theory of European Paleolithic art.

The theory essentially states that Paleolithic humans entered the caves and made the art to petition the earth to bring the animals to life so they could be hunted, killed, and consumed and human life could survive. Deep in particular caves, early humans sought for, found, and petitioned the animating origin of life with artistic images of animals they wanted to hunt, kill, and consume.

The cave was regarded as the origin of existence, and food and water needed for life were sometimes found there. Early humans entered the interior of the greater origin of life, the feminized earth. Earth was a place of the production of plant and animal life needed for food. Human artists, in a sense assisted the earth by seeding or impregnating it with the images of the animals they wanted to come to life, so they could harvest and aggressively hunt and kill them for food. The artists, probably mostly women, acted as both petitioners and as midwives to assist the earth to bring to life the animals portrayed in the cave art.

The Paleolithic artistic behaviors expressed in the interior of the earth are a concern of the human triune soul, as a hunger for food and water, sex and the reproduction of life, and aggression. By drawing and sculpting animal images on the cave walls, early humans were petitioning the earth to bring the animals to life so they could be hunted, killed, and eaten. The Petitionary-Midwife Theory of European Paleolithic art is a way of explaining the early human behavior of placing images of animals in the caves.

Entering the cave was an act of worship of the origin of animal and plant life. Humans saw a similarity of the female physical body with the material body of the earth, and thereby identified the origin of plant, animal and human life to be located within select underground caverns. The sculpting of the animal outlines and painting of the images in the caves is a combined artistic and religious endeavor. Humans accessed the origin of life through entering the cave. Paleolithic peoples were correct in that the origin of life is the supportive earth. As the female origin of life, the womb chamber was accessed by entering chosen caves.

Today the real origin of life is also recognized to be located within the material earth but not so much only in caves but the whole surface and the interior finer particles of atom and electron energy. The concealed energy located within the material earth, is continued in the unseen animating triune force within the human body. The essence of life is connected to the supportive material earth, and within the gross form of the earth to the energy particles of which the animating soul of life is a continuation.

Religions that revere and recognize the environment of earth and sun to be the origin of life are correct. Early humans who entered the caves of the earth sought to better explore and appeal to the origin of life. Exploration by prehistoric humans within the caves of the earth, is a precursor behavior akin to later historic religions that correctly emphasize empirical observation and exploring within the human brain and body.

Philosophical and psychological religions such as Buddhism and the Hindu practice of yoga explore the interior conscious self, and the less conscious and subconscious animating soul functions. The practitioners of these disciplines who explore functions inside the body, of sensations, picture images, and willing, will come to see they are connected not to a first father god but to their nearest relative, the real environment of the earth, sun, and energy dimensions.

Heretic Pharaoh

During the last third of the Bronze Age, circa 3500-500 BCE, a truly astounding event occurred in the land of Egypt. The actions and words of the Egyptian pharaoh Akhenaton (circa 1385-1335 BCE) became a precursor of the God-Soul Theory. Akhenaton ruled Egypt for seventeen years. The changes he brought to Egyptian religion, while provoking conflict in the culture, were relevant and praiseworthy then, and continue to be in modern scientific times.

The religion founded by Akhenaton, can hold its head up high through the millennia, far above the first father god of monotheistic religions. Modern humans can better approach reality by recognizing the religion of Atonism (Atenism) and bestowing proper praise upon this precursor of modern atomism and energy.

Over 3,300 years since the time of Akhenaton, the God-Soul Theory follows in the prescient and insightful Egyptian pharaoh's footsteps. Akhenaton was presciently antagonistic toward the accepted artistic visual depictions of gods and goddesses of his time, as well as any word portrait stories of them. Akhenaton achieved his goal, at least for a brief time, of ridding the Egyptian culture of the artistically imagined and portrayed gods with human attributes.

His decisive actions suggest that he correctly perceived that the gods and goddesses of his culture were imagined artistic products made only by humans for humans. His behaviors suggest he knew the gods were artistic metaphors for a nonhuman origin of existence and events. Egyptian artist-priests imagined and artistically portrayed popular human-like gods. The subjective imagination of artistic priests made the human-like gods and goddesses that did not exist based on any objective observation or vison of an external realm. Some gods were composite, mostly human-like in appearance but some had animal features such as a falcon head or the head of a hyena. An artistic small statuette of the worshipped deity was kept in the temple, the house of the god. The image of the human-like god was kept in a special darkened room in the temple, generally accessible to only a few, usually priests and members of the royal family.

As if real, the sculpture of the god was often bathed and dressed in linen, and adorned with gold and silver jewelry. On festival days, the statuette was placed in a small boat or ark, and carried on the shoulders of the priests through the streets in a public procession. Guards and musicians accompanied the throng while burning incense. The event was an artistic expression of drama for the public. The festival was a time to please the god and to plead for order of the environment, fertility of the soil, and a bounty harvest of crops. To entice public participation during the festival and artistic drama, the people were given loaves of bread and jars of beer.

The worshipped gods are often portrayed as carrying an ankh, a symbol of long life or eternity, and the artist-priests were associated with having knowledge and were able to provide answers to situations of life and death. Desire and envy for this knowledge attracted the interest of the average person, and so individual attention is given to the artistic portrayed gods and the priests who have knowledge of them.

Egypt built a great civilization of grand architecture, sculpture, and paintings of wall murals and hieroglyphs. The Egyptian culture also effloresced in religion, reaching its highest level of comprehension with the perceptions and practices of the pharaoh Akhenaton. Akhenaton called the sun the Aton, a name that may have been derived from the ancient Egyptian word jtn, meaning sun. The religion of Akhenaton was worship of the sun as a natural form of real radiant energy of light and heat, and not a word portrait of human artistic imagining. While the Aton was portrayed in stone wall sculpture, the art portrays what is observably real to all and not what is merely imagined by artist-priests to be accepted by adherents on blind faith. As for where things come from, Akhenaton did not prefer human-like gods and goddesses but rather a real natural object, the sun that emanates light and energy to benefit humans and all of life.

In stark contrast to the Egyptian human-like gods, there was no priesthood for Aton, only the pharaoh Akhenaton who deemed himself to be the son of the Aton.

Temples built to honor the Aton had no roofs and were open to the sky; there were no human-like sculptures and no dark inner chambers as in traditional temples. No offerings or donations to artist-priests were required.

In a written work attributed to or at least approved by Akhenaton, the prescient pharaoh mentions the benefits of the Aton, the radiant orb of light, life giving energy of the sun and radiant warmth, equally shared by all peoples and lands. There is one place all comes from into existence, and it is not a first father or a human-like god. Akhenaton perceived the forceful will-like radiant energy of the sun to be the origin of life.

The Aton is portrayed in low-relief wall sculpture as a convex sphere with rays of light emanating, at the end of which are opened helping hands. Depicted at the end of the rays coming from the sun are open hands that suggest giving of the magic-like touch of light and warmth that brings into existence the animating tendrilled growth of plants and sustains all of life. Two of the rays are often depicted with an ankh, the symbol of eternal life. The ankhs are at the end of a sun ray in front of the faces of Akhenaton and Nefertiti.

Flowing from the rays of the sun the depiction of the ankh suggests bestowal of the soul (Egyptian ka) of eternal life to Akhenaton and Nefertiti. The animating soul is a continuation of what was unknown at the time, the particles of energy of atoms and electrons from the earth, the element essence which is a continuation of the sun or Aton.

The animating soul within the living body is a continuation of energy elements of earth and sun. The animating soul of life derives its unseen resistance to destruction from the energy particle elements of the earth that are a continuation of the atom energies of the sun, the Aton. The soul, a forceful dynamic of hunger for food and water, sex and reproduction, and aggression, is a continuation of the energy particles of the environment.

Today it is known that the sun is a furnace of elements of hydrogen and helium that radiate energy and force.

The sun is visibly portrayed, while minimalist artistic representations of it depict rays coming from it as a way of making nonvisible energy and force visible. There was some minor anthropomorphism of human-like hands at the ends of the sun rays or beams, placed there to depict the helping benefits of the sun to humans and all of life. Akhenaton praises the Aton, the cause of the many effects that are real and observable for all to see, unlike the imagined art and story of human-like gods. The Aton is visible and real, accessible, and functions to benefit all.

For the population of the time, and continuing with popular monotheistic religions of today, to not have a supernatural human-like god means there is no assistance and no miracles. Without artist-depicted human-like gods, priests would then be out of a job of responding to needy people asking for assistance and answers. Who better to consult than priestly artists who possess the artistic images and words of a god, and have knowledge of and are closer to the gods. Having no human-like gods means no supernatural assistance, only natural benefits of the environment. This is just too much for average dependent persons looking for direction and assistance in life and death. Like the priests continue to do today, the artistry of the Egyptian priests provide an answer to the problems of life for a price, a tax, donation, or offering.

Religion combined with verbal and visual art, is a way of providing answers to deeply felt existential questions about life and death. The priests provided imaginative and false artistic answers of images and abstract word portraits of stories, and conducted rituals as ways to assist worshippers to obtain assistance from the human-like gods.

In the fifth or sixth year of his reign, Akhenaton declared that the traditional artistic sculptures, paintings, and verbal depictions of human-like gods and goddesses would no longer be tolerated and worshipped. Instead, only Aton, the visible sun and its energy would be worshipped. The changes Akhenaton brought to the Egyptian culture lasted but for a brief time following his death. Political and religious machinations combined with the ever-prevalent gullible peasant population, soon put a swift end to his clear communicated comprehension.

During his lifetime, Akhenaton was regarded by religious priests and the public to be a heretic, someone who holds views that differ from the established and accepted religions of the time. Following Akhenaton's death, theistic priests wielded political power and influence to convince most common people and the leaders to return to the traditional artistic visual and verbally imagined gods and goddesses.

Akhenaton did away with the artistic depictions of traditional gods and goddesses. Instead, he offered for worship the Aton, the real sun. When depicted in stone wall sculpture, it was portrayed as a convex disk with emanating rays or beams of light.

The Aton or sun was minimally represented in sculpture or painting as it was observable by all in the real cycles of morning, noon, evening, and night of daily life. Words found in historic records attributed to Akhenaton, suggest that he realized the human-like gods of his time were merely artistic products and exist only subjectively. Art may represent what is external and objective, such as a portrait or landscape scene. Yet art more easily imagines subjective images, such as Santa Claus, the Easter Bunny, leprechauns, and modern abstract art.

For Akhenaton, there are no real human-like gods, and there is no fantastic first father god. His actions reflect a breath-taking clarity of perception that did away with the artistic visual and verbal representations of where the environment and life come from. While Akhenaton did not have access to science, he did have observational evidence untainted by artistic images. To advocate that life comes from the sun, is to roughly say life comes from the environment and energy. His observation based groundbreaking religion of the Aton, correctly excluded artistic human-like gods and also a monotheistic first father.

Akhenaton may or may not have written the Great Hymn to Aton. The following are excerpts from the only copy, taken from the tomb of a member of the court during the reign of Akhenaton. The Aton is praised as:

"Ruler of the circle and ruler of the disk…ruler of the sky, and ruler of earth…."
"You appear beautiful on the horizon,
Animating Aton, the bringer of life.
When you rise on the eastern horizon,
You fill every land with your beauty.
You are gracious, great, shining, and rise high over every land,
Your beams reach everywhere to the limit of what you have made.

…Though far away, your beams are on earth,
While you shine on all faces, no one knows how you move…."

"…When you set over the western horizon,
The land is in darkness, like the sleep of death.

People sleep in a room with body covered,
One eye sees not the other.
What is owned and placed under their heads for protection might be stolen,
The thief they would not see.
The lion comes forth from his resting place,
As do all creeping things that bite and sting.
Darkness is a shroud, and the earth lies still.
Who made them all rests beyond the horizon…."

When the sun sets beyond the horizon, darkness is the result and people rest in sleep unaware. Bad things come forth in the dark to cause loss of property, health, and life. Without the shining Aton, thieves come under cover of darkness to steal, fierce lions hunt and kill prey at night, and harmful snakes come forth to bite and kill humans such as the cobra and horned desert viper, and scorpions to painfully sting. Only the light of the sun removes these threats to life.

Akhenaton tells the Aton, the sun, that he Akhenaton "…came forth from thy body…." In other words, he came from energy and force.

Realizing this entitled Akhenaton to be both ruler and the only ruling priest of Aton. When Aton shines, all is well on earth.

"All beasts are content in their pasture,
Trees and plants flourish,
The birds fly from their nests,
Their wings spread out to praise thy ka...."

For ancient Egyptians, the *ka* was the soul, the animating essence of life. Death occurred when the *ka* left the body and it ceased to be animated and alive. In contrast, the monotheistic religions see the body as containing no animating soul, only an external animator of a first father god who must animate and resurrect the physical body of his peoples. Akhenaton's words suggest he perceived that the animating essence or *ka* of Aton was its real radiant energy, and that the human soul and life is a continuation of it.

"...Creator of life in woman,
You who make seed in man,
You sustain life in the mother's womb,
You soothe and quiet weeping children,
You give breath and sustain life of all you have made...."

The making by the sun is ongoing and continually supportive of life functions. There is no first father god who breathes life into humans, or of an angry separation as portrayed in the Genesis story.

Akhenaton's words convey the aesthetic beauty and truth of a nonhuman origin. For his efforts, Akhenaton should be rightly revered as a true prophet of modern times. His words of truth have, if but faintly, endured over the past three millennia and continue to be relevant. His words and behaviors plainly show that Akhenaton intended to remove all visual and written artistic expressions of theism and its human-like gods.

During his reign, Akhenaton had the names of the popular gods chiseled away. There is mention that he also removed the plural word of gods from the spoken and written language of his time. The motive for his behaviors had to be that he saw the human-like gods of his time as artistic imaginings. He preferred what was one real observable nonhuman origin.

People in most cultures and times have preferred their gods to be human-like and portrayed them artistically in sculpture, painting, and words. The current practice of monotheistic religions prefers to artistically portray a first father ancestor god only in word portraits of scripture. Akhenaton based his religion on observation and perception, not on artistic imagination and conceived ideas. Compared with Akhenaton's advanced perceptual clarity and praise of the Aton, the simplistic artistic imagining and word portrait of a first father god of monotheism seems crude and vulgar in comparison.

Akhenaton was far seeing and his perception of a natural origin is relevant to the findings of modern science. However, even scholars misunderstand the significance of his prescient perception of reality. Quite a few Egyptian scholars myopically comment that Akhenaton's efforts for religious reform during his time, was an attempt to get away from lower polytheism toward the higher glory of monotheism. Some even compare the Hymn to Aton with the biblical Psalm 104.

One of the few exceptions, is a scholar who appreciates the significance of Akhenaton's perception of reality, the well-known Egyptologist Sir Flinders Petrie (1853-1942) who made the cogent remark:

"If this were a new religion invented to satisfy our modern scientific conceptions, we could not find a flaw in the correctness of this view of the energy of the solar system...Not a rag of superstition or of falsity can be found clinging to this new worship...."

While he is correct about the verity of Akhenaton's words, Petrie does not elaborate on what he means when he says that superstition and falseness was eliminated. He does say that Akhenaton's words are an accurate precursor of modern science and the quantum particles and atoms and electrons of energy. Surely the superstition and falsity he refers to are the obscuring cloud of any polytheistic and monotheistic humanlike gods that are glaringly and refreshingly absent from Akhenaton's words about the real origin of existence, the Aton or energy of the sun.

Akhenaton's words continue to be relevant and important in that he throws off the shackles of artistic imaginings of human-like gods portrayed with sculpture, painting, and word portraits. For the masses, artistic imaginings combine with artistic visual and verbal expressions to dull clear perception.

Most Egyptologists and historians seem to have an impaired ability to perceive, and seem to lack courage to speak up about what the evidence suggests that Akhenaton truly wanted to accomplish during his lifetime. Academic scholars tend to see the meaning of Akhenaton's words through monotheistic lenses. The consequence of this prejudice is to make lame comparisons with a superior monotheism. Blind scholars characterize Akhenaton as struggling to lead his people away from the lower stage of polytheism to the higher truth of monotheism. This is an academic error, and a distorting delusion of an unforgivable magnitude.

Akhenaton sought to direct the attention of his people, to what is recognized only in modern times to be the true origin of existence, the energy of the environment. Why would Akhenaton want to lead his people further astray from many artistically imagined gods to the monotheistic imagined word artistry of a first father god?

Why stray from the more accurate perceived view of the Aton or sun energy to a purely imagined first father ancestor god? Judaism as does Islam trace the origin of life to a first father, and Christianity to the same father god and his son. Akhenaton traces life to the real earth and the sun. What a real refreshing difference!

Akhenaton was correct to revere the nonhuman-like sun, the Aton. Today it is known that the sun's photons of transient particle waves travel at 186,000 miles or 300,000 kilometers per second. The animating of life is a triune soul of hunger for food and water, sex and reproduction, and aggression, that functions only as a continuation of the particle wave photons of light, and atomic elements of energy of the earth; a cooled remnant that was once part of the shining sun. The essence of existence consists of ethereal and real photons and atoms of energy that have ultra nano amounts of mass and weight that are the origin and supportive basis of all material and living forms.

As Akhenaton's words of genius intuitively and correctly assert, no artistically imagined human-like or first father god need be inserted into the wholistic reality of an environmental energy process of life.

Art and Artless

Ancient India developed internal methods of brain and body exploration and observation, including meditation and yoga exercises of breathing and postures. In the Middle East, no methods of inner exploration of brain and body developed, only strings of words intoning obedience and prayers to an externally located first father god who dictated social commandments to be obeyed.

The religion of Hinduism utilizes various practices of yoga disciplines, and also the artistic image of the physical *lingam-yoni*, the stylized sculpture of male and female genitals to represent the energy and origin of human reproduction. Aside from this explicit sculpture that refers attention to what is real and existing, the Hindu gods and goddesses have been craftily, artistically and deceptively, imagined and fashioned by priestly word artists of the religion to visually, verbally, and through writing to bring the deities into existence.

More in the tradition of the Egyptian pharaoh Akhenaton, is the artless Hindu son Buddha (circa 623-543 BCE). Like Akhenaton, Buddha was a member of the *Kshatriya* ruler-warrior caste lineage, not of the Brahmin religious caste of priestly visual and written word artists who portray the popular gods and goddesses of Hindu religion.

Artless Buddha had nothing to do with the artistic products of polytheistic or monotheistic religion. He did not promote or encourage religious art or rituals to be performed for the gods. Instead, Buddha promoted practical moderate ascetic disciplines and brain and body meditations. This pragmatic emphasis was to focus attention and to better observe, examine, and learn about brain and body functions.

In this way, the man known as to history as Buddha reached a preternatural clarity of insight, and so truly deserves the highest human praise.

After six years of effort, Siddhartha Gautama woke up and was given the name Buddha, meaning awake or awakened one. How impressive to think that twenty-six hundred years ago, a human reached to such an elevated level of cognitive clarity. Even to this very day few can reach the lofty heights he managed to ascend to, and instead continue a daily unawake sleep of existence. Through study of what is known of early words attributed to him, a practice of meditative observation led him to clearly comprehend two main areas of human experience.

By not promoting acceptance of the Hindu gods and goddesses, Buddha seems to have awakened to the discovery that the gods of the theistic religions of his time were subjective artistic expressions and overlays of reality to explain events of the environment and life. He must have comprehended that the gods are artistic ways of explaining where the environment and life come from, and are ways of imagining and obtaining protection and care from the vicissitudes of living and dying.

He must also have come to see what the Hindu *atma* or soul is, and is not. He taught that the *skandhas* are *anatta*, not an eternal soul. The *skandhas* are the effects of an animating cause that continues through many lifetimes of rebirth. The Sanskrit word atma is translated into English to mean soul. Based on the Buddha's views, the five *skandhas* or body-brain functions are what a physical person is. Since these functions are *dukkha*, ill-fit-together and consists of parts that are dependently conditioned, and since the parts are *anicca*, continually changing, then these formations are not an eternal soul.

Physical Body (rupa)
Sensations (vinnana) of seeing, hearing, smelling, tasting, and touching
Feeling (vedana) physical and mental feelings of pain, pleasure, and neutral
Willing (sankhara) brain and body behavior
Perception (sanna) includes picture images of now, memory and imagination that also functions as conception, reasoning, and intuition

The following words are said by tradition to be the second talk by the Buddha to his five followers after his awakening.

The verse does not explicitly say if there is, or what an eternal soul is but only that the body, feeling, sensations, willing, and perception are not the eternal soul.

"At Benares, in the deer park was the occasion. At that time the Awakened One said to the group of five brethren: 'Body, brethren, is not the soul. If body, brethren, were the soul, then body would not be involved in sickness, and one could say of body:

"Thus let my body be. Thus let my body not be." But, brethren, inasmuch as body is not the soul, that is why body is involved in sickness, and one cannot say of body: thus let my body be; thus let my body not be.... Feeling is not the soul...Likewise perception, willing and sensations are not the soul... Now what think you, brethren, Is body permanent or impermanent? Impermanent, lord. And what is impermanent, is that good or ill? Ill, lord. Then what is impermanent, woeful, unstable by nature, is it fitting to regard it thus: this is mine; I am this; this is the soul of me? Surely not, lord." (Kindred Sayings, Vol. 3, No. 69)

These words attributed to Buddha do not specify there is no soul but only that the five body-brain functions are not a soul. This begs a question, if Buddha did not explicitly identify the soul, is there any evidence in Buddha's words or practices that suggest what the soul is that animates succeeding lives of rebirth or reincarnation?

The Buddha and his early followers were forest dwellers. To find a hint of what the soul is for Buddha and his followers, it is necessary to consider the practices of the early forest tradition and later Sangha or monastic tradition. The three prominent practices of the tradition are the ascetic disciplines of eating one meal daily, celibacy, and meditative compassion. These practices more than any purported utterances or teachings show evidence of comprehension of the soul. The forest-dwelling and monastic practices serve to point the way and to counter the forcible willing triune soul of hunger for food, sex and reproduction, and aggression.

Early forest Buddhism advocated a retreat from busy society to meditatively better observe brain and body functions, to learn about the conscious self and less conscious and subconscious soul. It is difficult to closely observe individual brain and body functions in the distractions of daily life. Distractions are many in interactions with family members, friends, coworkers, and fellow humans.

The Renaissance artist Leonardo da Vinci (1452-1519) made the cogent observation:

"If you are alone you belong entirely to yourself. If you are accompanied by even one companion you belong only half to yourself or even less in proportion to the thoughtlessness of his conduct. And if you have more than one companion you will fall more deeply into the same plight."

Leonardo is correct as a companion fills a hole or empty place as a helpful support. Yet the other person also halves the wholeness of time and ability to investigate and learn, and distracts attention from close meditative observation of self and soul. Over attentive to another, attention is halved and directed from self to the other individual.

The inventor Nicola Tesla (1856-1943) made the relevant statement:

"The pressure of occupation and the incessant stream of impressions pouring into our consciousness through all the gateways of knowledge make modern existence hazardous in many ways. Most persons are so focused on attention to the outside world that they are wholly oblivious to what is passing on within themselves. The premature death of millions is primarily traceable to this cause."

For many, the attempt to introspect internal functions of body and brain, is disinteresting, even boring, and borders on painful isolation. There is more interest in external distractions of relationships and possessions.

Growth of knowledge of self and soul is aborted to instead favor growth of will-of-the-wisp distracting sensations, fun, and pleasures.

Prior to the modern sciences, humans utilized the observational methods of focused attention known as meditation. Meditation is useful in better observing brain and body functions. This is true especially of early forest Buddhism that sought to find out what animates life, and what moves the environment as change, and the motion of the greater universe. To better know the self and soul necessitates a reduction of distractions of time idly spent with others.

The meditative observations of early Buddhism found that what animates life is not a first father god. It was observed that what animates life is the hunger for and the getting and eating of food and water. It was surely comprehended that sex reproduces and animates life. It was also observed that aggression protects life, and is also needed to hunt and harvest plants and kill animals and ingest them as food to maintain the animation of life.

To find relief from the discomforts of life, the Buddhist culture of India utilized meditation to explore and comprehend the dynamics of the brain and body functions. Through a consistent practice of meditation, each may come to observe the shifting sensations of the senses, and the ephemeral changing conscious picture images of the cerebral cortex of the brain, to be an overlay upon a driving force within the body as a hunger for food and water, sex and reproduction, and aggression. From this internal situation and that of a changing environment, comprehension and relief is sought from the discomforts and pains of living.

Complication

Life is usually a series of various complications, a word defined to mean:

"An intricate or confusing relationship of parts, a complex combination of parts that cause a difficulty or problem; a situation, event, or condition that frustrates. A secondary disease, disorder, accident, or adverse reaction that aggravates the original condition."

Living consists of experiences that are often frustrating as life consists of parts and conditions that contribute to personal problems and complicate experience. Obtaining and consuming food complicates living, as do acts of sex and reproduction, and expressions of aggression. Life is often difficult, frustrating, confusing, and problematic, replete with disease, disorders, accidents, and various adverse reactions that aggravate and complicate living.

Internally, a life that is animated by a triune soul, and of necessity is forced to pursue food and water, sex and reproduction, and aggression, must often disappoint, must be fraught with risks and perils of many kinds, and cannot possibly have a good overall outcome.

Wanting to uncomplicate life, some humans accept the artistic word portrait of a first father god to assist them in their efforts. Monotheistic word art is an attempt to uncomplicate living by identifying the origin of existence to be a first father god, and is a way to command and promote social stability. Monotheistic writings about a first father god are word art that identify the beginning of existence, and serve to promote ancestor worship and obedience to paternal authority.

The best and realistic way to reduce the complications of life is to stay physically fit, learn much, achieve financial security, and cultivate supportive relationships. The individual must educate, meditate, and moderate the animating triune soul, the eating of food, having sex and reproduction, and expression of aggression. Sensing the aesthetic beauty of people, places, and things, also brings some mild relief from the complications and tedium of living.

Life is a juggling act of complications in the areas of health, learning, acquiring and spending money, and relationships. From the beginning and throughout, life is a juggling act that seldom ends gracefully. The individual consists of parts, functions, or details that require continuing attention and must be kept in functional motion without too often missing or dropping them.

When attention is distracted, the juggler and the juggling act is affected.

The juggling of events is the continuing efforts to balance the complications of life, interspersed with tiredness and the needs for rest and sleep. To assist each individual juggler, monotheistic religions offer an artistically imagined first father god who assists in the serial juggling of life's myriad complications.

Monotheistic Peace

Monotheistic religions offer faith and belief in a first father god as a way to arrive at a semblance of personal peace. This is the Middle East and Western subjective way to a personal peace. Monotheism may bring peace by offering a simple and subjective way of knowing an unknown beginning of existence. The artistic imaginative idea of a first father provides care and protection during life and during a hoped-for afterlife resurrection of the dead. The god functions as a moral guide by issuing commandments, and by providing reward and punishment for earthly behaviors. The simple story of an ancestral first father god brings some individuals a modicum of peace and relief from the unpeaceful demands of daily life.

Life is not separate from the good and evil willing-like ways of the environment that is the origin of life, supports it, and frequently ends it through drought, flood, earthquake, volcanos, and extreme weather events. The willing-like ways of the environment evidence little mercy, and the immature cerebral cortex of the brain seeks for comfort in its origin, by imagining it to be a first father god. In this way, humans have learned to distract attention from the will-like forces of the environment and instead direct attention to the imagined willing of a first father god. The environment is real and merciless whereas in story an imagined first father god is portrayed to be merciful but only if humans obey.

Through a lack of correct knowledge (Hosea 4:6) of a first father god, many perish. Unfortunately, like the prophet Hosea, many accept a first father to exist objectively. Many hope for and rely on a subjective delusion, and by so doing unnecessarily place themselves in harm's way.

Many fail to comprehend that a first father god is only a subjective artistic word portrait, imagined and sculpted in worded story images, as a way to make known an unknown beginning and to provide care and protection.

The way for monotheistic religions to achieve personal peace is to accept that a first father god exists who will take care of the individual during both life and death. So, not to worry, the Big Boss is on the job. This ideation scheme is mere artistic imagining illustrated in a word portrait of scriptural story. The artistic word art of a first father god appeals to many as a pragmatic way to succeed, avoid pain, and to survive.

Supported by this subjective dynamic utilized in the daily effort to live and to survive, many will not easily relinquish the monotheistic delusion of a first father god. Monotheistic religions are subjective works of word art and to mistake them to be objective will always and forever be delusionary. Trusting in a first father god is to trust in what it really represents, the sexual reproduction of a long line of biological fathers.

The real cosmological task of finding personal peace is not to proceed through life directing attention to a first father god. The real task is to comprehend human behavior to be a continuation of the behavior of the environment. A further task is to develop and increase apperception and comprehension that a first father god is subjectively imagined in the cerebral cortex of the brain and is expressed as monotheistic word art.

For the many inept, a first father god is dangled above for their attention to be directed to, and they are urged to beseech the first father for care and protection during life and death. It is fervently hoped by troubled and helpless adherents that the monotheistic first father will make life better by assisting them, and who will make choices for them. Becoming troubled and tired from dealing with life, an artistically imagined and caring first father god is offered by uncouth and deceptive sacerdotlists to the needy as a way for them to find subjective comfort and care on a real uncomfortable and uncaring earth.

Jesus, the founder of monotheistic Christianity, is often referred to as the prince of peace. Unfortunately, he did not live or die peacefully. Aside from all the portrayed drama and theological litter, the death of Jesus serves only as a model and a metaphor for access to the real door of death. The message perhaps? Lasting peace in life does not exist, and can only be truly found in a passing away from it.

Since the early Christians were Israelites and Jews, the New Testament writers portray the physical body of Jesus as being resurrected and it was eventually taken upward to a heaven by the first father. The body was bought back to life on earth, and then airlifted by the first father to another dimension as there is no animating soul in Judaism. The soul of Jesus is not mentioned, only his biological life is important and real and was therefore saved. (Acts 1:1-2, 9-11) The first father god saved and resurrected the physical body as an animating soul was nonexistent.

Buddhist Peace

In the life of the average person, the areas of love, bliss, compassion, and even-mindedness are often limited to specific people, places, and times. A Buddhist meditation practice seeks to remove personal narrow limits and to increase the thoughts and emotions of:

Love
Buoyant Bliss
Compassion
Even-mindedness

The above qualitative experiences are usually limited to certain persons, places, and objects in space and time. Through meditation, individual visualizations, thoughts, and emotions can be increased and expanded from a narrow focus and limited expression.

Limitations of the thoughts and emotions of these qualities can be delimited, the limits removed, and made at least during meditation, unlimited.

Meditative practice can focus and direct thoughts and emotions to fellow humans, until conscious attention and the less conscious and subconscious are imbued. Imbuing conscious and subconscious with a directed increase of love, bliss, compassion, and even-mindedness, lessens limits and is elevating and uplifting. Meditation on and directing these qualities with visualized picture images or thoughts and supplementing with accompanying emotions, is a way of cultivating and promoting the conscious self and reducing the subconscious soul function of aggression that contributes to situations and emotions of the opposing qualities of hate, stress and struggle, lack of empathy, and overly attached for or against others.

Appearing in conscious attention, picture images derived from sensations form a seemingly never-ending stream, or resemble a continuing series of waves on the ocean. The stream of imaginal thoughts and emotions roiling through conscious attention are most often limited to emotions of worry, frustration, sadness, hurt, or aggression. Meditation can be utilized to observe the continuing series of image-ladened thoughts and emotions, like waves on an infinite ocean and background of timelessness.

The ability for imaginal thoughts of love in the brain are limitless. There can be created thousands of imaginal thoughts and emotions of love, endless and forever, limitless like waves on the oceans of forever. Likewise, with bliss, compassion, and even-mindedness. It is to be realized that visualized thoughts and emotions of love, buoyant bliss, compassion, and even-mindedness, can be repeated without limit as an effective way to reduce internal and external conflict with others and all living things. The practice reduces and replaces the all too prevalent opposites of anger and hate, stress and anxiety, lack of empathy, and partiality of attachment and dislike of differences.

Meditation and Balance

Striving to learn and to live a better life, the cerebral cortex of the brain both reasons and imagines as ways of improving human experience. In times past, to counter the challenges and sufferings of life, monotheistic word artists imagined and utilized words to sketch stories of a first father god.

While objectively false, the word portrait of a first father god is subjectively fortifying to many, even though the verbal and written word art is barely clung to with a mere flimsiness of faith and trust.

Those living in western countries often consider meditation to be escapist and a waste of time, and by this attitude shirk personal responsibility of examining self and soul by appealing to an artistically imagined first father god, who all-knowing will take care of everything in life and death for the lazy and less curious. So not to worry, each knowledge-limited member of monotheistic religions can rest easy by believing there is a first father god to do the greater thinking for him or her.

Meditation is a long advocated, pragmatic, and proven practice of cultivating balance in life. Meditation practice has long been utilized to focus and reduce attention to distracting sensations of life, to reduce a stream of picture images of the conscious brain, and to reduce and balance both conscious and subconscious willing behaviors.

Life is a daily struggle to find balance within the brain and body, with the outside environment, and with other humans. Each must struggle to comprehend how to best live, and yet many fail miserably at the necessary existentialist task of finding relative poise. Life then becomes a painful struggle and temporary pleasures are sought to relieve the pains of living. The harmful paths to balance in life taken by many, are short term pleasures of various addictions for food, legal and illegal drugs, possessions, and relationships. Many become addicted to substitute, shortcut, and temporary ways of finding balance. The good of death may be sought as a way of alleviating the pains of life. Lacking balance, some prematurely hasten death by a lack of personal care, and some act to carelessly or intentionally take their own life.

Balance can be developed by a meditative practice of focusing attention, of observing the distinct functions of changing sensations, picture images of now, past, and future, and conscious willing for or against.

A meditative focus of attention observes these processes and removes their vagueness and separates them into distinct functions. With perseverance, a consistent practice of meditation can lead to the deeply satisfying and uplifting personal balance of comprehending self and soul.

If fortunate to have the ability for such a rigorous task, personal balance can be developed by examining the dynamic of self and soul. Inside each person is a conscious self, located in the cerebral cortex of the brain, accompanied by subconscious midbrain and body function of an animating forcible willing soul of hunger for food and water, sex and reproduction, and aggression.

Focusing conscious attention during meditation, the meditator may observe passing sensations of the senses occurring in now time. The life of a seventy-five-year-old person consists of 2,365,200,000 seconds, and sensations of these evanescent moments change from moment to moment. Picture images may also be meditatively observed to quickly pass through conscious attention.

Then can be observed the less conscious and subconscious body functions, the animating repetitive willing of a hunger for food and water, sex and reproduction, and aggression. It is difficult for humans to experience balance when animated by a triune soul. The existential task is to utilize the conscious self to better comprehend and to moderate the less conscious and subconscious function of the animating triune soul. Experience of the real soul is not a blissful and peaceful experience. Blissful experience and peace occur in the brain and body only when the excess influence of the animating soul is reduced.

It is a difficult task to comprehend conscious brain functions, and to observe and reduce the less conscious and subconscious animating triune force of the midbrain and body. The soul dynamic truly complicates human life, and it becomes a deadly brew of personal dysfunction when combined with impaired intellectual abilities and a failure to examine experience.

However good are conscious intentions and efforts, these are always only one step ahead of the subconscious triune soul as it remains ready to wreak trouble and havoc for each individual.

Those who are serious about personal balance have a vision of a greater reality, and so become recognized as founders of religions, saints, seers, and philosophers. Balance must be developed with the true origin of life, the environment and other humans. Each is faced with a real challenge to find balance by living in a safe and uplifting environment, maintaining health and fitness, learning and education, creative fulfilling work, and getting along with family and friends.

Meditation

A practice of meditation is useful to focus attention and to observe the changing of sensations of now moments, , the change of now picture images, and past and future images, and change of willing for or against. Focus of attention on now sensations of breathing, slow and reduce picture images formed from sensations of the senses. This is a challenging practice difficult to accomplish without boredom or sleep setting in to disrupt and distract attention.

The cerebral cortex transforms sensations into picture images and usually a conditioned habit stream of them. The struggle to focus conscious attention is pushed aside by the strong conditioned stream of picture images, and by the less conscious and subconscious animating willing of the triune soul.

The most difficult task to accomplish during meditation is the attempt to consciously moderate the animating willful soul, a dynamic less conscious and subconscious willing hunger for food, sex and reproduction, and aggression. This task is almost insurmountable to all but a few dedicated individuals. The conscious self does not find an easy task when confronting the triune soul. The animating and willing soul seeks to survive and resists observation, and reduction of its forceful influence.

Meditation is a discipline of improving cognitive clarity and comprehension by the consistent practice of focusing conscious attention. A focus of attention is an effort to reduce distraction to sensations, and to reduce conscious picture images. Meditative focus of attention can then be applied to observing brain and body. The subconscious function of midbrain and body stimulate humans to make conscious choices for food and water, sex and reproduction, and aggression. Less conscious habits form to reduce calculations of conscious reasoning and choices.

When consistently practiced, the result of meditation is an increase of clarity and observant insight, of better seeing and comprehending brain and body functions. Meditation is a progressive process of reducing distraction of conscious attention to the body, sensations, feelings, willing, and picture images. For short times during meditation, they do not appear in conscious attention. Conscious attention can then better observe any background animating factor of life previously not observed and can then better comprehend what animates its existence.

The essence of life is the animating willing that is so difficult to calm and reduce. The triune soul is a pattern of willing for food and water, sex and reproduction, and aggression. The subconscious animating soul can only be calmed as it is a continuation of energy and a cosmological force. The individual must make peace with the animating willing force of the triune soul that is resistant to destruction.

The soul is a less conscious and subconscious willing pattern formed by what interests an individual. Prior to death, dying must be as peaceful as it can made to be, and is to not be preoccupied with sensations, not to hold onto picture images, and to reduce and calm willing so it is not carried over to re-exist.

Continuation

It is superficial for any individual to regard their conscious self to be the essence of what they are.

The conscious self consists mainly of passing sensations, picture images and willing of the cerebral cortex of the brain, and emotions of pleasure and pain, character traits, and personality.

The essence of life is the subconscious animation and function of the body, not its conscious knowing of picture images. Most individuals fail to recognize the essence of what they are as the subconscious beating of the heart, breathing, digestion, and the silent healing of injury and illness. How could humankind for so long overlook the dynamic essence of what each is, the animating soul that enables survival during both life and death. What continues to exist after physical death is the dynamic function of the body, the essence of living, the wanting to survive of willing for food and water, sex and reproduction, and aggression.

Based on anecdotal and experiential evidence, a sizable portion of the public have personally had near-death experiences, seen, heard or felt a deceased family member or friend, encountered ghosts, or have recalled past life memories of reincarnation. The individuals are personally convinced that something exists inside the human body that survives physical death. These numerous anecdotal accounts suggest that death may well be a transition to a another if not better dimension. Something there is, inside of life that enables it to exist and survive. This is an animating soul, a willing effort to have food and water, sex and reproduction, and aggression. Biological life is a continuation traced to the local energy of the earth that extends to a nonlocal cosmological force that ever moves the universe. A conscious free will is free to do or not do, while the will to live is a less conscious and subconscious effort of cellular function of an animating soul.

For human life, time eventually runs out and the physical body dies. The biological tie of life, is untied from a limited time connected to the material earth. Yet the essence of life is a continuation of the essence of the earth, particles and elements of energy that are resistant to destruction. The body recedes away from physical observed reality and its animating willing function recedes to the reality of energy particles of which it is a continuation.

The inner animating function of life is a continuation with what is outer, and at the time of death must recede back to where it originated from, a dimension of energy.

What animates the human body is a continuation of particles of energy and supportive elements. The conscious and subconscious movement of the body is a continuation of the particle movement of energy, of atom and electron elements of the moving and rotating earth. The motion of the earth is a continuation of momentum of a timeless cosmological force that moves a dimensional and spatial universe of time. All in all, a seamless flow of motion of life and death as a continuation of a sole cosmological force that ever exists on its own.

What is inside the human body and animates it, also enables it to survive death. What exists as the animating function of every cell of the body, is a continuation of the energy particles of the earth. Indwelling and animating the body as a continuation of the energy particles of earth, is a triune soul. Willing effort in living forms is a continuation of energy particles and energy elements of the supportive earth. The internal restless willing of life as a hunger for food and water, sex and reproduction, and aggression, is a continuation of the restless change of the environment, and the restless ever moving universe.

Life struggles with the external environment and with the internal animating soul. Internal conflict consists mainly of the cerebral cortex of the brain and its conscious willing efforts to rule and reduce the influence of the midbrain and body, the dynamic of which is the animating subconscious of the triune soul. Conscious willing of the cerebral cortex of the brain opposes and conflicts with the less conscious and subconscious willing functions of midbrain and body. Conscious willing can postpone or redirect but eventually must obey subconscious cellular willing in at least three main areas, hunger for food and water, sex and reproduction, and aggression.

The animating and subconscious willing soul, though enabling survival, is an evil of living and only the good of conscious knowledge can discipline and moderate it.

Utilizing knowledge by visualizing picture images of a better outcome in space and time and willing toward it, an individual can better balance life to a tolerable now experience.

Subsidence

An animating triune soul is a relative push and pull continuation of a nonlocal cosmological force of unbounded space and unending time, and a continuation of particles of energy of the environment. As a continuation of this process, the animating willing soul is resistant to destruction. Since the triune soul is resistant to destruction, it can only be made to subside in content and forcefulness. With meditative discipline of observing, and mild ascetic limiting of forceful hunger for food, sex, and aggression, the forcefulness of the willing soul may subside. Patience in meditatively observing the animating force of conscious willing may eventually be effective in its subconscious subsiding.

Though unthinking and subconscious, respect must be shown by the thinking conscious self for its subconscious animating and willing essence of life. The willful force of the animating triune soul can be observed to last until such time as an intensity develops through countless lives for a personal quest to better comprehend the contents and functions of self and soul. Increasing the meditative practice of observing the willing soul, its forcefulness may be observed to moderate and to eventually subside.

The individual, aware of a willing soul within, may tire in attempts to obtain what it must repetitively seek, mainly to find food to put into the body, to have genital sex, and an object or person to direct aggression toward. Conscious attention may then glimpse in this temporary loss of interest, a potential for modification to the forceful animating and willing soul. This is the uplifting way to an un-soteriology, the un-saving of the animating triune soul that is resistant to destruction. The animating soul needs not to be saved but needs to be unsaved from life and existence.

As a continuation of boundless space and unending time, the willing soul can be lessened in its ever urging for food, sex, and aggression.

The trajectory and momentum of the animating soul can be made to lessen and slacken to reach a poise. Through consistent meditative practice, a conscious glimmer may dawn to reveal a way to gradually reduce the powerful forceful presence. A way is found open to decrease its forceful willing for food, sex and reproduction, and aggression. The primal essence can be observed, gradually directed, coaxed to lessen and moderate. In this sense, as the forceful individual soul subsides, it is uplifted and may then be free of the circle of existence.

Real Relatives

Saint Francis of Assisi (1181-1226 CE) observed the environment to be relatives of humankind. In his song originally entitled *Praise of the Creatures*, or better known today as *Canticle of the Sun*, Saint Francis vacillates between the ideology of an artistically imagined first father god, and the true and real relatives of life.

Saint Francis refers to the sun as a "worshipful" brother, as are fire and the wind brothers to humans. The moon is a sister, as is water. Earth is both sister and mother. Whereas, in the Genesis Garden of Eden story, death was a curse from the god, Saint Francis refers to bodily death as a friendly sister from which none can run away from.

In the words of Saint Francis, these real and objective relatives are marginally subordinated to a subjective and artistically imagined relative of a first father god. Francis does not use the Latin word for a male god which is deus, and he does not use the vernacular Italian word for a male god which is dio. Francis uses the Italian familiar word for respect, signore, meaning senior, sir, and sire. The imagined god is referred to more as a familiar father figure which is fitted in with the real environmental relatives.

Unfortunately for Saint Francis, to appeal to and praise a good first father is not helpful as it is a mere ideology for the higher cerebral cortex of the brain. As a senior sire, the word signore, only represents the sexual behaviors of many forefathers.

The origin of life is not an imagined first father god but what the god as external animator represents, an internal animating triune soul of hunger for food, sex, and aggression that is a continuation of the real environment.

To tweak the clarity of what saint Francis of Assisi is alluding to in his canticle, instead of an imagined first father god, the nearest external relative is the real earth and its energy. The true origin of life is the nearest relative, the mothering earth composed of energy particles, in turn connected to a related nonhuman cosmological force. The animator of life is its nearest observed relative, the earth and the motion of the universe.

Mother Earth

Monotheistic word art of an almighty first father only requires acceptance, belief, and faith of the reader or listener. Monotheistic writings of a first father god are an artistic answer to the question, how did the environment and life come into existence. Those who advocate for a first father god, then get to stand in for him on the earth.

In the biblical Genesis story, a transformational origin of life from the earth is portrayed as occurring through the behavior of a first father. The real assemblage of life occurs on the inside of the body as a continuation of energy from the outside supportive earth. What truly transforms and grows life is a forceful hunger for food and water, sex and reproduction, and aggression. This is easily observed in microorganisms, plants, trees, all species of animals, and humans.

From a background of a cosmological force, energy particles assemble into material forms, and on earth support the assembly of living forms. A better way to locate the origin of existence is through sensations and picture images of the brain that reason and measure the way to the origin of the universe. This is the organized observational method of science. In contrast, a first father god is a way the cerebral cortex of the brain artistically imagines where the environment and life come from. Imagining a first father god, is the way humans simplistically comprehend what animates them.

The umbilical cord of life is connected to a biological mother who gives birth while connected to the animating, mothering, and supportive earth. The real maker of life is what the umbilical cord is connected to, the living birthing mother, the mothering earth composed of energy particles, and the animating motion of the greater universe. An unknown first father is only imagined to be lurking beyond the observed motion of the universe as a simple artistic way to identify what first gave it momentum. Monotheistic religions imagine that a first father god rules humankind but the real ruler is the almighty environment composed of particle energy, and a cosmological ground or field of nonlocal force inferred to exist supported by observation of universal motion. The functional working motion of the environment is real, while a first father worker is imagined word art and not real.

The umbilical cord of life is an animating triune soul of hunger for food and water, sex and reproduction, and aggression, and is a continuation of and connected to the energy particles of the earth. Only in artistic imagination are humans connected to a first father. Biological males are the real model for the imagined paternal god.

The real provider of the food of life is the earth. To say a blessing before a meal by saying thanks to a first father for the food, is to thank the male who hunts, farms the land and raises animals, or works and earns the money to provide the food of life.

Unless having worked on a family genealogy, most people do not remember male relatives much past their grandfathers or great grandfathers. The great unknown of previous male relatives is the fertile background where a monotheistic first father god is imagined to exist, and is portrayed in the word art of scriptures. The word script is defined as:

"A style of cursive writing, or a system of writing. The text of a play, broadcast, or movie."

Monotheistic scriptures are a style of writing about a first father or the adventures of those who claim to interact or speak for the god.

Monotheistic scripts broadcast dramatic moving stories or plays acted out by the headline star performer of a first father god. Monotheistic writings are word art, and a first father god is an artistic word portrait. The fictional literature has entertained many and continues to entertain through the years.

Behaviors

The behaviors of the environment are not laws. Laws are associated with humans or a first father god who commands laws imposed to limit human behaviors. Various energy particles behave in certain ways as do planets, moons, suns and stars, and galaxies, all exhibit behaviors observed by humans. Forces of gravity, electromagnetism, dark matter and dark energy, exhibit detectible behaviors.

These behaviors are not related to behaviors of a first father god imagined to exist at the furthest beginning of human existence, and portrayed in human artistic stories of monotheistic religions. Monotheistic religions are a prescientific failure to observe and ascertain that human behavior is a relative function of the behavior of the greater environment.

The Egyptian pharaoh Akhenaton (circa 1385-1335 BCE) with utmost clarity observed it to be true that life comes from the environment. Not accepting Akhenaton's realistic view, Europeans instead accepted the origin story of the monotheistic religions that human behavior is related to the behavior of a first father god.

Christian monks struggle to comprehend a first father god they accept to be objectively real, when the first father is a made-up artistically imagined word portrait. Less intelligent monks of the past spent their lives copying manuscripts of the Old and New Testaments that herald a first father god. The monks were under the delusion that what they were struggling with was the effect of curses from a first father and the original sin of separation from goodness of the god. All the while the monks struggled, unknowingly, with their cerebral cortex of the brain to discipline an animating soul that causes so much havoc for humankind.

Rather than an animating soul, the religions of Judaism, Christianity, and Islam see the human body to be cursed by an imagined first father for disobedience of putting a knowledge containing fruit inside of their bodies. The unauthorized fruit consumption led to the know-how of sex and reproduction, hunger for food every few hours, and aggression toward one's own body and that of others. This unbeknownst to the monotheistic religions, is the dynamic of an animating triune soul.

Today the divide continues with those who accept the existence of a animating spirit or breath and those who do not. The religions of Judaism, Islam, and some Christian denominations continue to say no to a special animating spirit from the god, and continue to accept a resurrection of the body. Some Christian theologians do veer more toward the truth of the perplexity of what animates life, when circa 200s CE they were influenced by Greek thinking of a psyche or soul. In the words of the Greek speaking Jewish evangelist Saul or Paul (1 Thessalonians 5:23) can be discerned the merging of the Genesis animating breath or spirit, and the Latin anima from the Greek psyche. Paul says a human has both a spirit and a soul located in the body. The Saxon-English word soul is related to the Latin anima and Greek psyche as what continues after physical death. I include the English and the Latin translations.

"May the God of peace sanctify you wholly; and may your spirit and soul and body be at the coming of our lord Jesus Christ."
"Ipse autem Deus pacis sanctificet vos per omnia: ut integer spiritus vester, et anima, et corpus sine querela in adventu Domini nostri Jesu Christi servetur." (Catholic Encyclopedia translations)

The Christian groups who accept an internal animation, also dualistically continue to accept the deluded orthodox view that the animating spirit or breath is completely under the control of a first father god who will at some vague time in the future, reconnect it to the resurrected body. A sizable portion of the general population think of themselves as spiritual rather than religious.

These individuals accept the experiential feel of their own life experience that they have a soul, and they are also open to the Greek and Hindu views of an animating soul. These average people are much wiser than any theologian and adherents of monotheistic religions.

Yet even these people continue to be deluded when they advocate for a good soul worth saving. The human soul is good for survival but is not good at conscious reasoning. It survives on its own, and is its own savior. The soul is really the problem of life as it is an animating triune force, a forceful willing hunger for food and water, sex and reproduction, and aggression.

Model Offer

The touted good will of a first father god is a mental model for humans to will good, as a way to love and to receive love and reduce fear of existence. Monotheistic authorities encourage individuals to direct their will to acts of goodness and obedience. By respecting a greater will, individual excessive willing is reduced. Yet if carried too far, individuals become sheeple and follow the will of sacerdotalist leaders who display to followers the word art portrait of an artistically imagined god. Repeated often enough to the vulnerable, troubled, and struggling, listeners are mesmerized with the idea and various subjectively comforting monotheistic rituals.

In reality, a first father is only a story character for the beginning of sexual reproduction. The god endowed humans with genitals and he must also be endowed with them as he made humans in his own image, (Genesis 1:26-27) and it was his own knowledge that humans obtained and utilized to have sex and to reproduce.

The offer of a greater will to help one's own will to go on in life and survive death, is irresistible to many faltering humans. The will of a first father god reinforces individual willing. Whoever worships a first father reinforces their own will to continue.

It is the human will to continue and to exist that is really worshipped. The imagined idea of a first father strengthens human willing by encouraging an individual to be strong as the god is said to be.

A better answer to the willful struggle of life is not to reinforce individual willing with the imagined will of a first father god. The god only represents the origin and willing of human sexual reproduction. The answer to life is to de-will, to reduce and moderate the animating triune soul as a willing for food, sex and reproduction, and aggression. In this way the motivated individual can exit existence.

Blanket and Cushion

A first father god is an imaginal security blanket. Once accepted it can cover an individual from cold days and nights on the earth. It can be used as a tarp to provide cool shade and protect from the heated times of passing days. A first father god is a security blanket made not with cloth but fabricated with words. A first father provides a barrier, a separation for humans from the environment, which does provide some basic minimal care and support for life to survive. Wrapped with the word blanket of a human-like first father, provides even more subjective security, care, and support.

What cold or hot person on the earth would refuse to accept the comforting warmth or shade of a blanket? Children often hide under blankets that provide security from an imagined boogie man. Frightened immature adults also find protection under a sacerdotalist provided security blanket fabricated with words into a portrait of a first father god.

A first father furnishes a thin superficial imagined blanket-like protection from real harms in the environment. Many there are who hide under the superficial blanketing words of a first father god to protect from what is scary in the environment, and to reduce inner anxieties and fears of disease, injury, ageing, and death.

A first father god is an artistic way of softening the hard experiences of living. An imagined first father functions as an ideational subjective cushion, that gives comfort to an individual's ass while sitting through hard times, and while traveling the rough roads and potholes on the sojourn of life.

A monotheistic god is an imagined cushion upon which to rest one's weary head when tired on the journey of ups and downs along the roadways and challenging encounters of life. For the vehicle of individual life, a first father functions as a seat belt and an airbag to be deployed and to protect from the sudden accidents and unexpected impacts of daily living.

Malfunction

Monotheistic religions attribute the lack of living a functional happy life to being cursed and banished from the paradisiacal Garden of Eden, or as punishment for wrongdoing. Life does not suffer from punishment by a first father god but life usually functions well for a time but it also often malfunctions, meaning:

"To fail to function, to function imperfectly, or irregularly; to fail to operate, work, run, or go properly or as intended."

Consisting as it does of parts, both environment and life randomly malfunction. The environment functions and malfunctions with floods, earthquakes, volcanic eruptions, and other natural disasters. Human life functions and also develops errors and malfunctions in areas of health, relationships, and reasoning. Existence consists of parts and of necessity must eventually malfunction.

The cognitive error of the goodness of a first father god is an imagined artistic story to identify the beginning of existence, and the origin of good and evil. A first father is also a way to appeal for relief from the many malfunctions of living, in an often-futile effort to restore function and balance in an all too frequent malfunctioning, uncaring and unprotected existence.

Help

The willing-like change of the environment is capricious; it is usually supportive and helpful to humans but can just as easily be unhelpful. Since the environment is often harmful, a helpful first father god is artistically imagined by some cultures and individuals.

An imagined help is better than no help at all. To say there is no first father god is to say no help exists. This can in turn contribute to helplessness and existential despair.

A first father god is crafted with words to artistically construct a genealogy, as a way to help humans better comprehend the origin of existence. The word art of story that describes a first father god, subjectively helps many who accept the idea to have hope. The monotheistic artsy ally helps many to survive harmful life experiences by inspiring humans to have confidence that their own less than optimal willing can be helped by a greater willing.

A first father is an artistic ally, a word portrait of good but the god is not so overly good that he refrains from the use of evil as an option to get humans to be good. The Genesis first father helped humans into existence but he then became very unhelpful by placing some of his knowledge in a fruit where humans did easily acquire it, and the god proved to be further unhelpful by cursing and banishing them.

As the ultimate maker of all things that exist, a first father god is a way of praising the good of existence but what about the many evils that also come from either the god's will or his knowledge? Evil, best defined as excessive force, is both harmful and helpful. A first father god can use his ability to will evil to hurt humans as a way to help them to be good. The god will resort to evil if he has to so he can persude humans to be and to do good. In this way, the excessive force of evil can be used for good. How good is that?

An artistic word portrait of a first father god is handy and helps many to identify and make known an unknown beginning of existence. The strong-willed god helps humans to exert willful effort to be good and helps them to refrain from the excessive willing of force and harm known as evil.

Adults see children as innocent and pure from birth, and that kids only acquire an ability for evil or excessive force from exposure to harmful and traumatizing experiences in the environment. This is false and what is true is that the essence of life is a forceful triune soul that unfolds potential for evils during the course of a lifetime.

To help children do good, some adults utilize the imaginal helper of a good first father, just like Santa Claus, to teach children to be good, to obey, and to inhibit the innate willful impulses of bad and evil.

Life Skills

The terse Latin statement made by the Roman emperor Julius Caesar, "Veni, vidi, vici," can be applied to life in general. Every individual enters the arena of life by being born, grows, matures, and learns to see how life is. The individual then proceeds to develop life skills with which to conquer the small and large challenges of life, and to live life as best they can.

The artistic skill of subjectively imagining a first father god is a way of identifying the origin of existence, and is a way of providing subjective care and protection. A first father is a subjective comfort, however, what is needed to get through life are real objective individual skills.

Real skills are needed in the daily process of gathering what is needed to get through life with enough to survive and to provide some comforts. There are four main skills that are useful for getting through life. Probably the most important skill to develop in life is to learn and to practice how to stay healthy and fit. A further skill is to learn much and acquire knowledge in preferred areas of interest. It is important to develop work skills and to earn money for financial security and leisure. Last, but not least, is the skill to develop quality family and friend relationships for mutual support.

To develop individual skills is an existential chore, and only a minority are up to the challenge. For many on earth, the most pressing individual need is to survive daily life. The average person is not aware of the greater cosmic chore of developing personal life skills, and many individuals waste valuable time that could be better applied to the task at hand. Only the cerebral cortex of the brain can take humans to what is good. It can accomplish this in three main ways.

It can subjectively and artistically imagine a first father god who is all good. It can invent tools, weapons, machines, and techniques through the objective trial and error learning of science. The cerebral cortex of the brain can also take humans to the good of better defining and exploring the self and soul through objective study and subjective meditation practice.

Deicide

During the prehistoric Paleolithic era, humans entered European caves circa 40,000-10,000 BCE, predominantly in France and Spain. For 30,000 years they entered select caves with the pragmatic intent to predominantly draw animals. In entering the caves, early peoples were making a religious pilgrimage to the interior origin of life.

The earliest notable convincing act of deicide was committed by the Paleolithic peoples who circa 10,000 BCE, did away with going into select European caves and drawing animal images. This behavior was probably based on observation and evolved comprehension of the male contribution to the reproduction of life. The artistic efforts of petitioning the earth to bring forth animal life and send them to be hunted and killed for food, eventually fell into disuse and was terminated based on a lack of participation. Evolving human knowledge in a sense killed the practice of earth worship and left only what lingers to this day, a sentimental affection for mother earth.

The pharaoh Akhenaton (circa 1385-1335 BCE) committed an act of full-fledged deicide. During his rule he forbade all Egyptians to use verbal names and visible images and perform acts of worship to the traditional artistic images of Egyptian gods and goddesses. Only the Aton, the real sun was worshipped during his time of rule.

The German philosopher Friedrich Nietzsche (1844-1900) predicted a future deicide with his well-known pronouncement, *Got ist tot,* in English, God is dead. His statement predicts the future demise of the practice of monotheism and its first father god of Judaism, Christianity, and Islam. This deicide will likely soon occur in the first century of the present millennium.

It will none too soon be accepted that a monotheistic first father god is an artistic image, and story portrayed as verbal and written word art. Human worship of the origin of existence is directed outward to an imagined first father. The god exists only subjectively in the cerebral cortex of the human brain, and as such the artistic word portrait of the first father story character represents the origin of human biological development and sexual reproduction of many generations. Worshiping a first father god is really worship of the cerebral cortex of the brain that can subjectively imagine and utilize words to artistically portray the beginning of existence.

Jean Meslier

Jean Meslier (1664-1729) was born in the French commune of Mazerny. He furthered his innate intelligence and education by studying Latin with a local priest, and later entered a Catholic seminary. In the year 1889, at the age of twenty-five, Meslier became the local abbe of the village of Etrepigny, (population today 258) located near the border with Belgium, in the Ardennes region of northern France. Here he served the parishioners for forty years until his death.

In addition to serving as a village priest, Meslier was also a philosopher at heart, a lover of wisdom. Aside from his daily duties serving the people of the small commune where he lived, he also found time to contemplate the tenets of his own Catholic religion, and life in general. Though serving as a priest, Meslier disagreed with the teachings of religion and Christian theology. He eventually dedicated the passing years of his life to uncovering and revealing some few grains of truth from the chaff of monotheistic religion and its teachings of a first father god, served up to the public as the origin of existence.

When Meslier died, a last testament and final confession consisting of four handwritten quill pen copies of a manuscript consisting of 2,000 pages were found. His confession was not directed to a first father god but to his friends.

He began his testament and confession with the words, "My cherished friends…." Since the time of his death, Meslier's writings have been given various titles including, *The Testament*, and the *Memoir of the Thoughts and Feelings of Jean Meslier*. His last confession was a testimony to what he had discerned about government and religion, and life in general. In the 1864 first published full edition of his work, the inscription of his own words read:

"On a part of the abuses and errors of conduct and of the government of men, where clear and obvious demonstrations are shown of the vanity and of the falsehood of all the divinities and all the world's religions, to be addressed to his parishioners after his death, and to furnish them with a testimony of truth for themselves and all their fellow human beings."

Throughout his life, the Meslier remained quiet about his personal views on the governing aristocracy and religion. Publicly revealing his views during his lifetime would certainly have resulted in punishment and even death. Only in his writings found following his death does he finally confess his true sentiments.

"How I suffered when I had to preach to you those pious lies that I detest in my heart. What remorse your credulity caused me. A thousand times I was on the point of breaking out publicly and opening your eyes, but a fear stronger than myself held me back, and forced me to keep silence until my death."

Meslier's last words as curate were for the future care and cure of his fellow humans. He suggests in much of his writing that the class role models of society as the dominant nobility of military might, and clergy with its emblematic first father god whose greater power they represent, and the role of submissive peasants, must be removed.

Meslier champions equality and friendship as a replacement model. His words seem to have influenced the values of what would become the national motto of France, "Liberte, egalite, fraternite," meaning, liberty, equality, fraternity.

His writings are a verbal tyrannicide and deicide in which Meslier argues that the governing aristocracy rules harshly and is uncaring and wants to have more power and wealth, and wants and to stand out and reign above as superior. Monotheistic authorities also want power and wealth and utilize the idea of a monotheistic first father god to obtain and dominate. Theologians and religious authorities, pretend to have knowledge of a first father god and emphasize the authoritative word art of theological scripture. The leaders of the governing nobility utilized their intelligence to organize and to dominate the populace. Monotheistic authority figures utilized their intelligence to write sermons, books, and develop rituals to reinforce the subjective artistic word portrait of a first father god.

The Catholic church promoted the artistic fiction and story character of a first father god, and often utilized it to abuse and dominate the populace. The nobility used force to maintain social order and to protect, and the church used the dictated commands of a first father god to instill order. Both nobility and clergy claimed authority to direct society and the individual to the good of order. The aristocratic government is superior in term of imposing taxes and amassing wealth, and superior in military and policing social order with force of arms. By representing a superior first father god, clergy also portray themselves as superior. All other humans are then deemed as not superior and are inferior.

On the earth an individual excels with either brain or body, and seldom both. Meslier's affection for the non-noble peasants, represents a rejection for the intelligence of the nobility and clergy who used intellectual talents for dominating the lesser intelligent and toiling peasants.

Meslier prefers what he subliminally detects in the peasants, the animating and willing soul of life, the essence of which is the growing, raising, obtaining, and eating of food, sex and reproduction, and moderate aggression to survive. He recognizes the often-harsh aggression and artificialness of the nobility and clergy, as perverting and abusing the natural growth and peasant behavior of life.

The dynamic structure and behavior of society can be seen to represent the dual physiological functions of the cerebral cortex of the brain and central nervous system, and the midbrain and autonomic nervous system of cell and organ functions of the body. For the governing nobility and educated clergy who emphasize the cerebral cortex of the brain and higher order, of reasoning and art, the peasants represent the less intelligent orderly dynamic of the soul that predominantly functions for food and water, sex and reproduction, and aggression. As do the midbrain and autonomic nervous system of the cells and organs of the body do for the cerebral cortex of the brain, so the peasants do the work of keeping the learned ones alive.

While government offers help and protection to society, as do religious authorities offer the imaginary help and protection of a first father god, the real answer to assistance and protection in life is alluded to in the opening words of his Testament, "My cherished friends…." Meslier's answer to the twin problems of the ruling nobility and monotheistic authority, is friendship and mutual communal support. Meslier's view of government is that it is often harsh and uncaring. The monotheistic god of Catholicism never acts to make life better for humans. This leaves the only reality of friends to be relied upon on for kindness and assistance during the journey of life. Meslier suggests the only real assistance, kindness and comfort that can be relied upon during the journey of life, exists in friendship.

Meslier's writings favor a verbal and behavioral tyrannicide of the ruling aristocracy and religious authorities, and the deicide of an imagined first father god that supports both. Probably the strongest words written by Meslier against the abuses of the tyranny of the ruling nobility and especially monotheistic religious authorities, are the following words:

"This reminds me of the wish that a man once made, who had neither great knowledge nor had he studied; but who, apparently lacked none of the common sense in sanely judging all the detestable abuses and ceremonies, which I am criticizing here. It appeared by the manner of explaining his thought, that he saw far and that he penetrated far through the mystery of iniquity, which I will speak of, since he recognized so well their authors and the troublemakers.

He wished he said, in relation to the subject I am speaking of, that all the great ones of the Earth and that all the nobles could be hung and strangled with the guts of the priests…It is short, but expressive; since it explains with few words that which these sort of people deserve."

Mesliers intense words inspired participants of the French Revolution, including Denis Diderot, who paraphrased Meslier's words by exclaiming: "And with the guts of the last priest, let us strangle the last king." For Meslier, monotheism is a symptom of ignorance and fear, and is a problem to be solved. Meslier says "ignorance and fear" are the two cornerstones of religion. The God-Soul Theory is in agreement with Meslier's view. The theory asserts that ignorance mistakes the monotheistic view of a first father god to be objective when it is really an artistic work of word art, and is therefore only subjectively real.

Ignorance is the ignoring of the dependence and origin of life from the earth, and instead substitutes the false and artistic genealogy of a first father. There is also ignorance of an internal animating soul that is ignored and forsaken for an external first father god. By a monotheistic preference for a resurrection of the material body, there is a forsaking of the metamaterial soul. The soul is metaphysical as it is a continuation of energy particles of the earth and sun, and is therefore resistant to destruction.

Fear is also the origin of religion, especially fear of the unknown. The unknown past is scary for both primitive and modern humans, so there must be an attempt to identify it in some way. The future too of what will happen next is unknown and often frightening. Life is a rush to get things done and each thinks they have plenty of time.

The reality is that time has each individual in its ever-changing natural sequences of days and nights and seasons, until at last it releases its unrelenting grasp. There is also fear of judgement by fellow humans for expressing doubt about the existence of a first father god.

Even Meslier mentions a "greater fear" held him back from sharing his philosophical musings with his parishioners, a fear of the great disruption his communication would cause to himself, friends, and fellow villagers. To express his views would have brought him great discomfort and even death for heresy. A good example of groupthink.

There is a fear on the part of individuals to not speak out on their own subjective skepticism and doubt on the existence of a first father god. Many accept the subjective idea of a first father god from fear of the harmful changes of the environment such as flood, drought, earthquakes, volcanoes, tsunamis, hurricanes, tornados, and weather.

Add to this animal and human aggression, illness, injury, and ageing. Lack of education breed superstitious fear. It is human fear and helplessness that uncritically accepts an offered helper from the clergy. Helpless fear produces a vulnerability and a gullibility to the offered spoken and written authoritative explanation of an unknown beginning to be a first father god. Acceptance of the idea of a first father may also be based on hedging one's bet that it is possible but not likely that a god exists. For many, just the idea of a first father reduces fear and may produce a good feeling of protection that is all too readily accepted through ignorance. A few of Meslier's insightful quotes on the existence of a monotheistic god include:

"Theology is but ignorance of natural causes reduced to a system...a continual insult to human reason."

"In truth, to adore God is to adore nothing but fictions of one's own brain, or rather, it is to adore nothing...In worshiping God, man adores himself."

The statements variously assert that a first father god only comes about through an ignorance of the environment. Having little data on natural cause and effect functions to engage reasoning, the brain instead imagines a supernatural god and portrays it to be the cause of existence. A first father god is indeed a subjective fiction, an artistic word portrait. The last statement suggests that the ego of a first father god is the inflated importance of the human ego.

Whoever follows a first father god, follows a bigger ego than their own, a Big Boss. A first father is imagined to be the organizer of the environment and life when really the god is how humans egocentrically organize their knowing about the unknown origin of existence for their own care and protection. In place of a first father god Meslier asks:

"Is it not more natural and more intelligible to deduce all which exists, from the bosom of matter, whose existence is demonstrated by all our senses, whose effects we feel at every moment, which we see, act, move, communicate, motion, and constantly bring living beings into existence, than to attribute the formation of things to an unknown force, to a spiritual being, a God?"

"Since it was necessary for men to have a God, why did they not have the sun, the visible God, adored by so many nations? What being had more right to the homage of mortals than the star of the day, which gives light and heat; which invigorates all beings; whose presence reanimates and rejuvenates nature; whose absence seems to plunge her into sadness and languor? If some being bestowed upon men power, activity, benevolence, strength, it was no doubt the sun, which should be recognized as the father of nature, as the soul of the world, as Divinity. At least one could not without folly dispute his existence, or refuse to recognize his influence and his benefits."

As Meslier suggests, humans do seem to have an innate curiosity, a cognitive necessity to question and to somehow identify where all things and especially humans have come from. However, the environment and life are natural miracles, not supernatural miracles from a first father god. They do come from a super nature of a sensed but only inferred unknown cosmological force, from which come the unseen transcending energy particles of atoms and electrons which transcend, and therefore shape material forms of the sun and earth.

A first father god is a superficial subjective idea of the beginning of existence. A first father is given credit for knowing how to make the environment and life.

The real maker of life is the supportive material earth, and its mass animating essence of energy particles of atoms and electrons of elements. The internal animating of life is a continuation of the earth, and is a dynamic willing hunger for food and water, sex and reproduction, and aggression.

Meslier writes that the idea of a first father is so feeble for the average person, human passions easily override any fears of the god. These innate "passions" that Meslier mentions but does not define, have to be what Meslier denies the existence of, the animating and willing triune soul of hunger for food and water, sex and reproduction, and aggression. On the existence of a metaphysical soul, Meslier suggests that like a first father god, it too is only imagined by humans. He conflates both a first father and a metaphysical soul to be false, yet only the god is an artistic imagined word portrait.

The idea of an animating spirit or breath has been added to the human body by some Christians denominations based on a few words attributed to Jesus, including "And Jesus said unto him, Verily I say unto thee, Today shalt thou be with me in paradise." (Luke 23:43) The words suggest something exists within the body of the thieves and Jesus that transits to an afterlife dimension. In Judaism there is a lack of an animating soul and the body must be reanimated by a first father god. The accepted use of a first father god by Christians, seems to also serve as a pragmatic artistic word portrait that represents the transition to another dimension.

Meslier extrapolates that since a first father does not exist, so the popular view of an animating soul is nonexistent, and like the body so too the soul is "material and mortal."He relies on his own reasoning and also invokes the argument testimonies of classic authorities such as Pliny, that the soul is but the material and mortal function of the body. Meslier insists there is a failure to identify the substance or presence of the soul. He also suggests the soul is a mere metaphysical fancy and a desire to escape physical death.

"The existence of another life is the imagination of men, who, in supposing it, have but manifested their desire to live again, in order to enter upon a pure and more durable state of happiness that that which they enjoy at present."

Meslier is correct in his view that a first father god exists only subjectively and does not exist objectively. While I agree with Meslier about a first father god being a subjective idea, I must disagree with him about his insistence on the nonexistence of an animating soul. Deicide is a deserved good, but Meslier's suggestion that the animating soul of life is nonexistent is an egregious error.

For Meslier, it makes sense that since a first father god is a literary fiction, and that the body is material, then an animating soul that enables survival must also be a fiction and be material as well. Yet unknown to Meslier at the time he lived, environmental material forms and living forms, are just an outer shell composed of an inner animating of energy particles that are resistant to destruction.

In his writings, Meslier encourages supportive mutual friendship which is certainly a benefit to survival and enjoyment of life. Friendship also points to a shared dynamic of living, and indirectly points to a mutually shared animating triune soul as a willing force of hunger for food and water, sex and reproduction, and aggression. There is an equality of the subconscious animating soul, inasmuch as all that lives must eat food and drink water, have sex and reproduce, and display verbal and physical aggression.

Humans are equal in having a subconscious animating soul that seeks to willfully survive life. The inequality of life comes from the content of the cerebral cortex of the brain, the conscious self. The content of the cerebral cortex of the brain makes the qualitative difference between the ruling aristocracy and monotheistic authorities, versus the peasant population. Both the ruling aristocracy and monotheistic authorities, like their first father god, aspire to rule with a higher intelligence that differs from the less intelligent, undereducated, and lowly peasants of the countryside. Peasant intelligence in turn dominates the lesser intelligence of the animals.

Inequality is the essence of what Meslier investigates in his writings. Meslier prefers the peasant population over the nobility and clergy. For Meslier, the nobility and clergy are elitist, disingenuous, domineering, and at times cruel and tyrannical. Yet the peasants, while basic and down to earth, are undereducated, superstitious, brutish, and often barbaric.

Meslier devalues the affluence of the nobility, and the clergy's use of a super hero first father god, intended to dominate and inspire the peasants to obedience and better behaviors. Many answer the call to come be in the presence of a super will, fabricated with words and presented by clergy as an artistic portrait of a first father god. The image of a first father is made by mere words read and spoken by clergy. A first father god is a fabrication, a word art portrait upon which to focus attention as a way of knowing human origin and obtaining care and protection.

The assembly of people in a group, a mass, is a real-time fashioning of a super will of mutual cooperation and strength. The mutual getting together, Meslier suggests, should not be a directing of attention to a subjectively fabricated icon of a first father god. Getting together should be an opportunity and occasion to demonstrate mutual respect, tolerance, compassion, and willing love of friendship. Yet living or meeting en masse, often leads to conflict between and among individuals, and a consequent lack of amity is the result. This is superficially solved by clergy manipulating the populace with the word art of a first father, and the peasants agreeing to accept the artistically fabricated word portrait of the god to be the common human origin. Alleged written willful commands of the god are communicated and are expected to be equally obeyed by all.

The basic existential problem of life for all classes and each individual is the conflict and tension between them caused by the animating and willing soul. Regardless of class differences, each is in a hurry to have the next meal, to have sex and reproduce, and with words and behaviors to express aggression. This is the animating triune soul and is the real essence of life and death.

There is a struggle of classes, the nobility and clergy versus the peasant population. Unbeknownst to Meslier, as per the God-Soul Theory, this outward class struggle has its roots inwardly. The struggle between good and evil, is between the cerebral cortex of the brain (monotheistic god story character) and the midbrain, spinal cord, and body (Garden of Eden serpent, later Satan, Devil) the dynamic of which is the animating soul.

The undereducated conscious cerebral cortex of the brain is a problem for humankind. There is also the problem of a less conscious and subconscious midbrain and body dynamic of an animating soul. Both are a barrier to conflict free friendships. The soul consists of a real problematic forceful willing to relieve a recurring hunger for food, sex and reproduction, and aggression. The bad behavior of the ruler and nobles, and monotheistic religious authorities, complained about by Meslier, are an expression of the animating soul, the real trinity of life.

A first father results from the conscious willing and picture image ability of the brain to use words and story to craft the origin story of a god. The first father god of Genesis is a mythical genealogy, a way to identify the origin of existence lost in a distant past of almighty time. For monotheistic religions, artistic imagining suffices to identify the origin of existence. The cerebral cortex artistically imagines and fashions a god as a pragmatic tool, and as a way to control and dominate the environment and to command and control humans en masse. Carefully considering its advantages and pragmatic benefits, the intelligent elite of European culture, the ruling aristocracy and monotheistic authority, adopted the word art portrait of a first father god.

A mention exists that Meslier expressed a wish that after his death he wanted to be buried in his garden. Following his death, and upon examining his written work, church officials were shocked and displeased with Meslier's topics in his writings. The officials interred the curate's body in his residence garden and in an unmarked grave. Having no tombstone to mark the spot, its exact location is unknown today.

In the eyes of the ecclesiastical authorities, to be forgotten is a fitting punishment for Meslier's sacrilege of writing heretical words against the nobility and clergy of the Catholic church. Fortunately, his writings survive to serve as remembrance.

In his devotion and search for psychological truth, Jean Meslier is a true saint of the Catholic church yet he will not ever be recognized as such. The conclusions he reached about monotheistic religion, demonstrates intelligent insight and an ability for accurate perception and apperception of the utilitarian subjective word-built first father god. However, his view on the nonexistence of an animating soul of life is not correct.

Facade

The evils of life and the excesses of the soul in its efforts to survive, are the raison d'etre for the artistic word story of a first father god. Monotheistic religions are a poor artistic attempt to solve the mess of willing that is life. The stronger will of a first father is imagined to control human ability for willing, a will bestowed upon them by the Genesis dualistic willing good and evil god.

If a limited human cerebral cortex, and there are many, cannot comprehend a problem of life, then it can appeal to a higher intelligence promoted by monotheistic authorities. Sacerdotalists make an offer to individuals that many cannot refuse. The offer is a way to bolster individual willing by directing attention to and having faith and trust in the stronger willing of a first father, and imploring the god to willfully act on one's behalf.

An artistic word portrait of a first father is an imagined backup upon which to call during threatening times of life. The traits of a first father serve as a protective umbrella. The god who makes and knows all things is said to be omnipotent and omniscient. With the added trait of omnipresence, of being everywhere, then the unknown is less to be feared, and an individual can be guided and protected wherever they may be.

The way monotheistic religions attempt to both strengthen and to reduce the strong human individual willing ego, is by imagining the greater ego of a first father who made the immense environment. The first father god is imagined to will good things for humans but he also can and does will evil toward them. The Christian first father wills a lake of fire, (Revelations 20:15; 21:8) a willed greater evil awaiting after death to punish and torture the willing evil done by humans during life.

This is a monotheistic metaphor that human evil willing, will encounter a greater amount of and ability for evil in the future. The lake of fire to torture an individual eternally, is a metaphor for the internal heated passions of the human willing soul that is resistant to destruction. The story metaphor is a comment on the animating triune soul as a forceful willing for food and water, sex and reproduction, and aggression.

To say the will of a first father god always exists, is a half true statement. Real willing exists but a first father god only subjectively exists. To say a willing exists that is resistant to destruction and therefore tends to always exist is true but it is human willing and not that of an artistic imagined first father god. Human willing tends to always exist as it is a continuation of energy particles from the environment, and is resistant to destruction. A first father is an ideational façade that eclipses the greater environment composed of energy and material form. A façade is defined as:

"An artificial and deceptive surface, the main front of a structure."

A first father god is a façade, an imagined artificial surface to define the origin of existence. A first father god is deceptive as it is only subjectively real and does not exist objectively. A first father god is a super official as the human erected superficial main front of the structure of the vast universe and the environment and life.

Images of a god, whether of sculpture, painting, or portrayed with words, orient human attention to locate the cause of an event, such as where did the environment and life come from.

A monotheistic first father god is a rallying cry, an imagining of greater intelligence to rely upon and to utilize in proceeding through an often disappointing and dangerous life. An imagined intelligent first father is the valorization of a non-intelligent and forceful urge of reproduction that produces the ills and evils of life. The forceful urge of sex is irrational and the impetus of a rational first father is a way of rationalizing and accepting sexual reproduction and its consequences. The imagined face of a nonsexual first father god is a disguise of sexual reproduction, an intelligent sanctioned reason to proceed with daily life.

Emotions and thoughts of dying and death are often disorienting. To know there is a long line of sexual reproduction, and that so many others have previously died, and others including oneself will die in a future time, is what prompts many to accept the nonsexual origin of a first father god. The intelligence of a first father legitimizes, sanctions, authorizes, and justifies the inability of human intelligence to control sexual reproduction.

A rational first father god is an imaginary externalized model of a greater and pure reason that compensates for the limited internal and often impure reasoning ability of the cerebral cortex of the human brain. Worshipping a first father god is a way of ascending from a lower human rationality to a higher rational level of reasoning, and of increasing conscious human knowledge. This psychological projection is a way of appealing to a greater rationality and of overcoming the irrational subconscious human soul.

In the Genesis story, the first man was made by a rational intelligent first father, not from an irrational force of the sexual urge. This is a way of valuing the intelligent cerebral cortex of the human brain by use of the artistic word art of story. The intelligence of a first father god is a way of valuing the human cerebral cortex of the brain over the midbrain, genitals of the body, and sexual reproduction.

Monotheistic religions insist that only a first father god who has ideation can enable human survival after death when what really survives is the non-ideating and willing individual soul.

In the book of Genesis, the free will of humans is portrayed as being inserted into the first human with an animating breath from above by a first father god. Au contraire, the animated willing of life is inserted from below, from the soil of the material earth. Molecules of the physical soil and water of the earth are organized to form life by the metaphysical particles of energy and various elements and minerals of the earth. It is this natural process that is given the guise of a supernatural first father god in story. A nonsexual first father made humans without having sex, from the soil of the earth and a rib. Yet the first father god also made humans in his image (Genesis 1:26-27) with, of all things surprising, dormant genitals later activated by humans from knowledge of sex made available and placed within easy reach by the god, and acquired by humans from the fruit of a special tree.

Sex can make more life but cannot save it from dying. Only an intelligent first father knows how to make and save life. If the origin of life is accepted to be intelligent and makes life, then it must know how to remake life from residue scraps of bone and dried flesh from a long dead body; hence a resurrection. Intelligence did not make life; a non-intelligent continuation of energy animates and orders and disorders life supported by the material earth.

The human body is mortal but its animated willing is resistant to destruction. Monotheists give credit to the willing of existence by a first father god and denounce and defame human willing. In monotheistic religions, the first father's will, is what bestows continuance of life during a resurrection of the human body and a restoration of its willing and of breathing or spirit.

Human willing is a real continuation of energy and a cosmological force that is resistant to destruction. Human individual will, is not recognized to be special or metaphysical in any way, and is really defamed by imagining a dominant super will of a first father god. Only the first father is accepted to be metaphysical. Human free will came directly from the animating breath of the god, yet its metaphysical quality is unrecognized.

That there is a metaphysical presence within humans is what Jesus points to in some of his words but his insight is muddled and obscured by the traditional artistic metaphor of a first father and a resurrection.

In the Garden of Eden story, a free will was breathed into the body of the first human by the first father god. The animating breath of a free will is the alias of an animating soul. The willing soul is metaphysical, is not composed of the material physical soil, but comes from the energy particles that compose the earth and as a continuation thereof is resistant to destruction. The will, alias the soul, is not rational, it is irrational, less conscious and subconscious, exists for survival, difficult to direct, resistant to destruction, and relies on and is guided by knowledge. This is recognized in most religions of India that give credit to individual willing known as karma that must be reduced and resolved as it is resistant to destruction.

Holy Spirit

Use of the Christian term "holy spirit," began to be used during the 100s and 200s CE. The term holy "ghost," as explained by the Catholic Encyclopedia, is the Old English word *gast* defined as breath, a synonym for the Latin *spiritus* meaning breath. The Encyclopedia also authoritatively states that use of the term holy ghost "is not the proper name" for one-third of the trinity.

Accepting the words of the Genesis story (2:7) of the first father breathing into the body of the first human to animate it, early Christians began to think of the god's spirit or breath to be coequal to him as an activating substance. Eventually, Christians accepted Jesus to be the begotten son of the god, and added him to the mix to arrive at the construct of the trinity.

The primitive metaphors in the second chapter of Genesis reveal an overlooked and important truth. The first father is a metaphysical god who breathed the metaphysical substance of his breath, certainly not an ordinary breath, into the first human's physical body and it then began to willfully move and live.

The god did not utilize his spirit or breath to breathe into animal forms, so this suggests that it is a special metaphysical substance intended only for humans. The first father god breathed his metaphysical breath into the nostrils and body of the first human and animated it to freely and willfully move and live. The clumsy story metaphor of an impetus from the first father that animates life within to willfully move, points to a real metaphysical animating function, that is passed down during sexual reproduction.

The mentioned metaphysical breath of the god did not just stimulate the human body to breathe and then remain external to the body, it had to join with and animate every single cell and organ of the body to move, function, and continue to live. At the time of death, the biological breath of the body ceases, and the metaphysical spirit or breath of an animating free will departs, leaves the parts of the body to die. A first father is said to be metaphysical and to exist forever. Since humans received a metaphysical animating breath of a free will from the first father, they too can in some way exist forever.

From his metaphysical form, the first father god exuded his spirit or breath to animate the first human. Biblical authors of Genesis failed to see a significance of the first father aspirating the inert body of the first human with his metaphysical spirit or breath. This observation was not lost on early Christians who paired it with some of the words of Jesus about humans surviving physical death of the body to enter an afterlife dimension. (Luke 23:43; John 14:2)

Christian theologians consider the god's spirit or breath to be an active function of the trinity, the three-in-one godhead. Following death, the human spirit or breath returns not to the metaphysical body of the first father but to his externalized spirit or breath located in the vicinity of the god.

The animating spirit or breath of human life comes from the first father, and upon death, returns not to the form presence of the god but to his holy spirit, in a sense the externalized reservoir of the god's breath surrounding and existing near yet distinct from him.

The rarified spirit or breath of the first father may have eventually been associated by Christians with a dimension of heaven where the human animating spirit or breath transits to exist in the ethereal spirit breath of the god.

When the Genesis first father made the first human and breathed the free will of life into him, (Genesis 2:7) the god must also have endowed the man with some basic intelligence as he could soon give names to the things that he first saw. (Genesis 2:19-20) Later written gospel words of Jesus suggest that following death, the animating breath or spirit retains a person's intelligence and a basic personality and memory of deeds to be judged. In writings associated with Judaism, Jesus was the first to mention "many mansions" (John 14:2) or dwellings of an afterlife dimension. Especially during Christmas, Christians honor the son of a first father who as his coequal will save them from death by providing an afterlife dimension in which to dwell. Prior to Jesus, only a hoped-for resurrection of the body was available.

The words of Jesus suggest that individual intelligence is active and survives death. For Christians, human intelligence remains imbued in the individual metaphysical spirit or breath when it returns to be near the greater intelligence and spirit breath of the first father. The animating human spirit or breath returns to the holy spirit or breath of the god. For Christians, the first father's spirit or breath is a metaphysical essence or substance. For Jewish rabbis, the metaphysical spirit or breath of the god is just a stimulus for the first human to breathe, and the metaphysical substance does not infuse, permeate, and survive biological death. This is a major difference between the two monotheistic religions of Judaism and Islam, and the religion of Christianity.

The god's holy spirit is his exhaled life-bestowing breath that must also surround his presence. At the time of human death, breathing stops, and Christian theology suggests the animating spirit or breath returns to its origin of the first father, to the metaphysical spirit or breath substance exhaled by and surrounding the god. For Christians, the exhaled spirit or breath of the god began to be known as the holy spirit, the metaphysical breath of the god.

The holy spirit must be a reservoir of the first father's breath, and may have become in time the afterlife dimension of a heaven, where the animating spirit or breath of the individual goes to reside in the holy spirit or breath of the first father. This is a primitive metaphor based upon physiological breathing of the human body, its ceasing, and its seeming departure at the time of death.

The Holy Spirit or Big Breath, is a metaphysical effluent or essence from the first father god. The god also visits humans and inspires them with his spirit or breath, he breathes visions and dreams into them. He also inspires humans to have an attitude, of a high or low spirit.

A first father god and his nonvisible animating spirit or breath, are story metaphors for the environment and the not visible energy particles that compose it. The animating spirit or breath of imagined story is a metaphor for a real animating soul that is a continuation of particle energy of the environment that is resistant to destruction. What is externalized and attributed to a first father god's spirit or breath as an ability to animate and resurrect the body, occurs internally as an animating soul of willing for food and water, sex and reproduction, and aggression that is resistant to destruction. Supported by and as a continuation of the external environment, the life bringer is an internal animating triune soul.

For often helpless humans, it is better to be in the hands of a subjectively imagined intelligent and good first father. To observe that life is a continuation of the environment and contains a real forceful triune soul that is resistant to destruction, nonintelligent and most often out of control, is not a good thing to acknowledge.

Since humans disagree about what is good, the artistic word portrait of a first father ancestor is offered and accepted by many as a way of promoting general agreement on what is good. The imagined god represents the reality good of the higher cerebral cortex of the brain and the lower midbrain and body pleasure of sexual reproduction that brings life into existence.

The task of life then becomes plain to sight, which is to direct conscious attention to what is good but since reality of the earth is both good and evil, there is always a daily risk of disappointment and despair.

If another dimension exists, then it must be natural and has nothing to do with a super natural first father god. The real saver of life is not outside as a good first father but is inside, and it is not good. The not so good saver of life is an animating triune soul composed of ninety percent subconscious willing hunger for food and water, sex and reproduction, and aggression, and ten percent of conscious intelligent reasoning using picture images of objects in space and time.

Undying

Monotheistic word artists offer individuals a way to survive life and death by portraying the origin of existence to be a first father god. The cerebral cortex of the brain helps humans to survive by subjectively imagining a first father helper. The first father is an image applied with words to the extremis terminus of time and biological reproduction. The pain and horror of disease and dying produce confusion, and subjective relief is sought in imagining and artistically using words to portray an undying first father god. An imagined undying helper is the subjective way of surviving a nightmarish existence of struggling through a life that must eventually end in death.

Sacerdotalists claim to have knowledge of an external undying essence they identify to be a first father god who gave life to humans. An undying essence did give life but it is an animating willing triune soul of hunger for food and water, sex and reproduction, and aggression. The soul is a continuation of real energy particles that bestow a resistance to destruction.

To identify a real undying essence, human gaze must cease to look outward based on monotheistic story, and instead attention must be directed inward to a silent animating function.

That an undying essence exists within the human body must somewhat be accepted on faith and belief as only cells, organs, muscles, and bones have been observed to exist within the body. The reason for this is that the soul has not been correctly identified. While a higher intelligence is given credit for helping humans to survive, it is really a nonintelligent earth and a less intelligent, less conscious, and subconscious animating soul that helps humans to survive. A real undying essence external to the human body, has only recently been identified by science to be force and energy.

The force, field, or ground that moves the universe must be undying, as are particles of energy according to the theory of conservation of energy. Environmental force and energy exists within living forms as a continuation, as an animating triune soul of a willing hunger for food and water, sex and reproduction, and aggression. The animating willing soul is good for survival but causes many of the problems of daily living that include the numerous and varied abuses of food, sex and reproduction, and aggression. Conscious human willing of the cerebral cortex of the brain is a continuation of subconscious willing function of the body cells and organs, that is a continuation of the willing-like change of the environment and energy particles.

The outer material appearance of the earth consists of inner particles of energy. Like humankind's closet relative, the earth, the physical human body is composed of inner molecules and energy particles that function as a dynamic animating and willing soul. The body is the outer form of an inner animating dynamic willing soul, a forceful trinity of a hunger for food and water, sex and reproduction, and aggression.

Episteme

Within the human body, the ancient ageless and undying function is not a breath or spirit from a first father god but is an animating and willing urge for food and water, sex and reproduction, and aggression. The soul is a continuation of growth from the energy particles of the environment.

This shared origin is the basis for the bond of socializing, to have fun, to mutually relieve the animating tension of the willing soul. The triune soul is the glue for the stickiness of social interaction for better or worse.

Monotheistic religions do not recognize humans to have a soul, a few only an animating breath or spirit, and others only a physical body that is said will someday be resurrected. In chapter two of Genesis, biblical word artists sketch the story of a first father god who exhaled an animating spirit or breath into the first human. The first human then willfully moved his earthly body to live. This must also have been the occasion of receiving a free will, to do or not to do.

The existential chore of life then is to will more good than evil, and to acquire more good and less evil knowledge. Difficult to do since the first humans inherited a good and evil will as well as knowledge from a first father god. Yet humans continue the daily struggle to avoid evil and obtain what is good in life.

Hindu seers are not quite as deluded as the word artists of monotheistic religions. Hindus at least recognize the existence of an animating *atma* or soul. The existential chore is to remove from this life the accumulation from past lives of negative karma or *kleshas*, meaning clouding emotions or afflictions of fear, anxiety, jealously, and sadness that cover over a blissful essence of life. Those with karmic afflictions keep reincarnating until they are removed and the good karma of yoga and meditation reveal the blissful good *atma* or soul within.

This is a nice carrot to pursue, and is at least better than a goofus monotheistic body resurrection, or having an animating spirit or breath from a first father that returns to the holy spirit or breath of the god until he reattaches it to the resurrected body. It is a great sin of separation from reality and from what is true, to say the essence of life is a good first father god (monotheism) or that life contains a blissful inner essence (Hinduism).

Legend claims that when Buddha experienced awakening, he reached down and touched the earth. The legend explains that he did so as the earth served as the only witness to his accomplishment. It must be noted that Buddha did not imagine and thank a first father god for his accomplishment. The behavior of touching the earth may be seen to be a profound gesture, a recognition of the true origin of life as a continuation of the animating energy particles that form the soil and water of the very real earth. Forest living and meditation advocated by Buddha, brings to attention the prominence of the strong forceful triune urge of hunger for food, sex and reproduction, and competing aggression. This animating willing dynamic is observed to exist even in plants that contain the triune animating essence of growing life.

Buddha revealed a realistic way to bliss that comes by reducing the forceful willing soul that causes reincarnation. The dynamic force of willing for sensations and picture images of food, sex and reproduction, and aggression, must be observed and gradually reduced through mild to moderate discipline. The methods are the training of attention to stillness through meditation. The practice of yoga postures contributes to train the body to hold still in position, and thereby promote relaxation and stillness of attention.

Curate

A curate is defined as a person who is tasked with the care and cure of souls. In this sense, defining what the soul is, then each individual is better equipped to care for and cure his own. To develop soteriological knowledge of how to save an individual from the soul, attention must be trained and directed to decrease conscious willing by a focus attention to the continual change of sensations and picture images.

Meditative conscious attention comprehends that sensations are too brief, as are fleeting picture images. Intelligence, following due diligence of meditative attention, training and observation, may eventually comprehend that conscious willing is often brief, frustrating, disappointing, difficult to direct and maintain effort, and has uncertain outcomes.

Conscious willing efforts contrasted with inexhaustible time are relatively and ridiculously brief. Cognitive processes of sensations, picture images, and conscious willing may then lose some of their allure, and may become more amenable to discipline and focus of direction.

Non-meditative persons are usually addicted to sensations, and as a consequence fixated on picture images. Meditators reduce sensations by getting to a quiet place and closing the eyes. The meditator reduces picture images of now objects by closing the eyes, and focusing attention to slow and still picture images of past memory and future images. With practice the meditator reduces boredom and does not fall asleep.

Human conscious willing can accomplish many good things through both art and science. To increase good willing over bad is the real challenge and problem of life. This is so as conscious willing of the cerebral cortex is affected by subconscious willing of midbrain and body functions. Bodily hunger stimulates the cerebral cortex of the brain to make picture images of food, sex stimulates picture images of a partner, and aggression elicits picture images of a person or object.

The living body is fragile and subject to injury but as a continuation of force and energy, the animating willing soul is resistant to destruction. Human willing is long term resistant to destruction and is fueled by ephemeral sensations and picture images, of wanting to do, be, or to have. Nourished by sensations, and picture images, willing can continue forever. Observing moment to moment change of sensations, and picture images, and willing for and against, willing can be reduced, relaxed, and resolved to a relative restful poise.

Sensations rapidly change and should not be clung to, as well as picture images of now, past, and future. Conscious willing for housing, cars, clothing, and vacations, change through weeks, months, and years, and should be only relatively clung to. But the core essence of life, a subconscious soul of willing for food to reduce hunger, for sex and reproduction, and for aggression, is resistant to destruction.

Only meditation and the training of attention to focus, observe, and to comprehend can cure the willing soul. This accomplishment brings uplifting joy and peace, and a preference for the experience. It brings more lasting satisfaction, and when developed soon comes to be preferred, rather than the common repetitive exercise of excessive, obsessive, and often frustrating willing for food, sex, and aggression.

Unsaving Self and Soul

Humans want more of their favored conscious sensations of seeing, hearing, smelling, tasting, and touching. Yet since sensations are brief, change from second to second, and do not endure for any length of time, they are really not worth having. There must be a practice of not having them, of letting them go.

Meditation is a practice of observing and training attention away from sensations of:

Seeing
Hearing
Smelling
Tasting
Touching

Picture images exist only briefly, they do not endure for any length of time, and are not worth having. There must be a practice of not having them, of letting them go. Meditation is a practice of observing and weaning attention away from picture images of:

Now
Past
Future

The way to preserve sensations of experience is for the brain to utilize them to make picture images in a spacetime sequence. Since sensations last only briefly from moment to moment, and picture images made from them rapidly appear and disappear, willing effort for the sensations and picture images of food, sex, and aggression must be moderated.

The essence of life, the triune soul of willing for food, sex and reproduction, and aggression, is often troubling, frustrating, uncertain, and may result in emotional and physical injury and death. Therefore, the animating willing soul is not worth having. There must be a practice of not having it, of letting it go. Meditation is a practice of weaning attention away from the animating willing soul by observing and moderating the triune force of:

Hunger for food
Sex and reproduction
Aggression

Willing effort can last longer than either sensations or picture images, and exists in conscious attention and less conscious, and subconscious functions. Sensations exist for only moments, and picture images of now, past, and future continually change moment to moment, they have little intrinsic value and have only extrinsic pragmatic value of orientation in the environment. Since sensations change they are not worth much. This is also true of picture images of now, past, and future. The willing shifting effort to have sensations and picture images is also not worth much. But since the effort of willing is resistant to destruction, it cannot be destroyed, only reduced in intensity to mild and moderate. Hunger for food, sex and reproduction, and aggression, can be reduced and moderated but cannot be removed as the triune soul function is the metaphysical essence of life.

Meditation is the overseeing and developing of not wanting to have of sensations, not wanting of picture images of now, past, and future., and not wanting to will for or against something. A saint is a person who reduces willing of the triune soul to a moderate minimum. The accomplishment reduces frenetic activity and bestows conscious and subconscious ease and poise. Each must save himself from the real animating willing soul; an imagined god can only subjectively save an individual. The impetus for life is a continuation of energy particles and an accumulation and accretion of organic molecules.

The individual triune soul is resistant to destruction as it is a continuation of atoms and electrons of the environment and a greater sole cosmological force of the universe.

There are a lot of word stories written about a monotheistic first father god but there are no stories about an animating soul of life or how it functions. Some Christian groups accept an animating spirit or breath that contains a free will, intelligence, and survives physical death. The animating spirit or breath is given and controlled by a first father from which it came, and who will one day reconnect it to the body during a resurrection and final judgement. The undereducated and untrained person prefers the easy way to be saved with little personal effort except for some faith or trust in the traditional word portrait of a first father god and indulging in various rituals. Such silly superstition.

The real task is to learn how not be mortal again, to be amortal, having no death, to not want to have, or be in a body, or have a body again. To be without a death is to be without the inner animating dynamic of a triune soul as a hunger for food and water, sex and reproduction, and aggression. A triune soul cannot form a living body but may be able to join and animate a developing fetus to result in reincarnation as a dynamic continuation of particle energy that prefers a circular motion. For those who investigate this dynamic, there must be an individual effort to resolve deep roots of subconscious willing functions, and conscious willing for picture images of objects in a spacetime sequence.

Conclusion

Monotheistic authority figures have long ruled western society with the flimsiest word portrait of a first father god. The notion of a first father has had a two-thousand-year hold on the ideation of humans. Only in the modern twenty-first century is the obdurate idea finally being relinquished by humankind.

Throughout this work, the God-Soul Theory has been applied to the tenets of monotheistic theology.

The theory argues for a psychological view of semi-atheism, meaning, a first father god is subjectively real to a good portion of humankind but in no way, can the acceptance and beliefs of many insure that it is objectively real. A monotheistic god is a prescientific way of identifying an unknown beginning, and is a subjective imaginal or artistic way of orienting to what is good and protective of humans in a real, good and evil environment. Imagining a first father is a way of stabilizing internal emotions and worries, and a way of controlling what is external. The first father god of monotheism is derived not from reasoning but is a product of artistic imagining and word art in an effort to know an unknown beginning of the environment and life.

The God-Soul Theory asserts that a monotheistic first father god is an expression of human ability for artistic images portrayed in word art. Therefore, the popular conceived notion of a human soul cannot have been made by a first father god. An animating soul is a continuation of energy and force.

If the soul can be said to be caring, it cares only to exist and survive as befits its sole attribute of having a resistance to destruction. The soul is a triune force that functions as a willing hunger for food and water, sex and reproduction, and aggression that animates life to survive. An animating soul is a continuation of the natural environment of energy and it is this factor that renders it resistant to destruction.

Perplexed by life, and its continuing forceful hunger for food, sex and reproduction, and aggression, and eyeing the progressing discomfort of daily life, some humans seek comfort by regressing to a past beginning of an all good time. A first father god is an artistic attempt to turn attention to what is good, a maneuver that occurs only subjectively as images of word art in the cerebral cortex of the brain. Goodness is accepted to be located in a first father god but is actually located in the good pleasure of sexual reproduction by a series of real biological forefathers.

The comedian Rodney Dangerfield while tugging at his tie during his monologue, often repeated his famous line that so many can identify with, "I tell ya that's the story of my life, I don't get no respect."

Applying this amusing comment to monotheistic religions, it is a first father god who gets all of the respect, while the animating soul of life is not even recognized and gets no respect at all. If the presence of an animating soul is recognized to exist in popular folk monotheism, it is not recognized for what it truly is. A few monotheistic religions, including Catholicism and several Protestant denominations, accept that humans have a surviving spirit, an animating breath not a soul, that survives death but it must someday be reconnected to the physical body during a resurrection. For the average person or folk monotheism, a person does have a soul that must be saved by a first father god, or by his son.

The imaginal idea of a first father exists only subjectively in the cerebral cortex as scriptural word art. An animating soul is real and is not related to an artistically imagined monotheistic god. The soul needs no savior as its existence is saved by being a continuation of the energy particles of the environment and a sole cosmological force. The physical body is animated by a metaphysical soul. Its origin and roots are a continuation of energy particles and atoms of the supportive earth.

The conscious cerebral cortex of the brain can discipline the less conscious and subconscious midbrain and body dynamic of the animating triune soul. Yet the cerebral cortex must also respect the dynamic functions of midbrain and body willing that is the animating soul of life. The respect accorded the willing of an imagined external first father god, must instead turn attention inward and transfer respect to a real internal animating soul of the midbrain and body, the dynamic of which is a willing hunger for food and water, sex and reproduction, and aggression.

A hyperopic respect for the willing of an imagined first father god, must be corrected to focus attention and clear comprehension on the near and interior real animating dynamic of a less conscious and subconscious willing soul. Respect must be demonstrated for human willing that enables an individual to survive life, and as a continuation of energy particles of the earth and cosmos, respect for the willing soul to also survive the death of the body that it animates.

The less conscious and subconscious soul survives as it is resistant to destruction. The conscious self assists survival the only way it can, by artistically imagining and manufacturing a first father god. A first father is a subjective way an individual disengages and extricates from objective problems of existence such as where did the environment and life come from. When encountering real problems of life, the subjective idea of a first father easily accompanies and supports an individual when dealing with objective threats. The supportive subjective idea of a first father god is available when sooner or later each individual is made aware of vulnerability to helplessness, fear, injury, loneliness, poverty, and ignorance.

That a person has received from a first father god a supernatural spirit or breath is a poor metaphor for a real animating soul as a willing hunger for food and water, sex and reproduction, and aggression. The soul does not come from what is higher and from above but is a continuation of what is lower and below, from the energy particles of the supportive earth and surround environment.

The animating of life and its willing to survive as a hunger for food and water, sex and reproduction, and aggression, have come from particles of energy of the earth that are resistant to destruction. The first theorem of thermodynamics or conservation of energy states that forms change and are destroyed but not the energy of which they are composed.

Speculating as to percentage, a surviving soul consists of what is least desirable, consists perhaps of ninety percent less conscious and subconscious forceful urges of hunger for food and water, sex and reproduction, and aggression. Surviving residual picture images comprise perhaps ten percent of the conscious willing soul. The content of conscious knowledge of the cerebral cortex consists of picture images.

The content of subconscious knowledge of the midbrain and body consists mainly of habit and repetition, such as digestion of food, sexual arousal and reproduction, and fight or flight of aggression, and also includes heartbeat and circulation and breathing.

This is the subconscious knowledge acquired by the first humans from the family genetic tree, and is the knowledge cursed by the first father god character of the cerebral cortex.

The subconscious knowledge of the animating and willing soul consists of habits, repetition, and reincarnation. The existential task is to clean up the triune soul that is resistant to destruction, and that is littered with countless less conscious and subconscious picture images and willing urges for food, sex, and aggression. A meditative disciplined effort calms attention to sensations, to picture images of now, past, and future, and calms forceful willing of an animating triune soul to reach minimal expression. Akin to an ever-existing sole cosmological force, an individual soul returns to merge and blend with its origin.